Advance praise for *The Working Mom*

'Vicki is one inspirational mumboss, who shares her secrets to juggling a thriving business with raising a family in this entertaining and empowering read'   **Una Healy**

'If ever there is a person who has shown just how successful you can be online while also being an amazing parent it is Vicki. Read, learn and follow. A brilliant book from an inspirational mother'

Natasha Courtenay-Smith, author of *The Million Dollar Blog*

'*The Working Mom* is a must-read for any woman looking to balance a career with motherhood. Packed with insights into building a strong digital brand, delivered in Vicki's typical down-to-earth style, the pages radiate her passion and enthusiasm for business and life. This is a woman who seriously knows her stuff. An inspirational and empowering read'

Andrea Thompson, Deputy Editor, *Marie Claire*

'Accessible and inspirational, Vicki Broadbent is a mumboss who delivers candid, practical advice with authority and warmth'

Julia Bradbury, television presenter

'For any woman who is wondering how on earth you are going to be you and a mum all at the same time, this book offers reassuring, witty and practical tips to make the most of both your job and your baby. A must-read for the modern mum, particularly one who has aspirations to build her own business. I wish I had been able to read it three years ago!'

Katie Massie-Taylor, Co-founder, Mush

'Full of practical advice for anyone ready to create a living on their own terms – this is a brilliant, empowering book'

Jessica Huie, MBE

'I loved reading *The Working Mom*. Just because we become mamas doesn't mean we lose all our career goals. This book is a must-read for all mums trying to juggle life, work and kids'

Sarah Willingham, entrepreneur and former dragon on BBC Two's *Dragons' Den*

'If you want to know anything about how to make it as a #mumboss, Vicki is your go-to woman! In her true down-to-earth style, Vicki manages to combine practical tips and tricks with personal anecdotes to help you win at work and home. A must-read for all women wondering how to successfully navigate career and children'

Nikki Cochrane, Co-founder, Digital Mums

'A must-read book from the pioneering Vicki of Honest Mum, *The Working Mom* is a blogging and vlogging handbook for budding and experienced bloggers alike. Brilliant'

Susanna Scott, Co-founder, BritMums

'Inspiring, motivating and a bloody good read. *The Working Mom* is not just a blogger's bible – it's a confidence-boosting kick up the backside for anyone wanting to juggle creativity, entrepreneurialism and parenthood' **Sophie, Tired 'N Tested**

'A fantastically honest read for all mums ... inspiring'

Maggy Woodley, Red Ted Art

THE WORKING MOM

YOUR GUIDE TO SURVIVING AND THRIVING AT WORK AND AT HOME

VICKI BROADBENT

PIATKUS

PIATKUS

First published as *Mumboss* in Great Britain in 2018 by Piatkus

First published as *The Working Mom* in North America in 2020 by Piatkus

1 3 5 7 9 10 8 6 4 2

A CIP catalogue record for this book
is available from the British Library.

ISBN 978-0-349-42395-1

Typeset in Albertina by M Rules
Printed and bound in the United States at LSC Communications

Piatkus
An imprint of
Little, Brown Book Group
Carmelite House
50 Victoria Embankment
London EC4Y 0DZ

An Hachette UK Company
www.hachette.co.uk

www.improvementzone.co.uk

ABOUT THE AUTHOR

Vicki Broadbent is the founder of honestmum.com, one of the UK's top parenting and lifestyle sites, and an award-winning TV director and filmmaker. She has written for a range of publications, appears widely on TV and on panels as an expert commentator, and creates content for global brands. Vicki has also written online for publications including *Marie Claire UK, Good To Know, Grazia Daily, Woman* and *The Huffington Post.*

Vicki won the BritMums Brilliance in Blogging Awards in the Outstanding 'Best of the Best' Category in 2016 and also in the Social Media Category. Her film work was awarded the Channel 4 4Talent Award for Best Director amongst other awards, and she was a finalist at the *Red* magazine Red Hot Women Awards. Vicki was also a finalist in the Creative Entrepreneur category at the NatWest Great British Entrepreneur Awards 2017.

Vicki regularly gives keynote speeches and contributes to discussion panels about blogging and running an honest lifestyle brand. She has spoken at *Marie Claire*'s Future Shapers Live and The Advertising Internet Bureau, and she founded a workshop with Jessica Huie MBE entitled 'Turning Passion into Pounds', which launched in collaboration with *Stylist* magazine's #Reclaimyourlunchbreak campaign and the British Library.

To my kids, who made me a mum and a boss

CONTENTS

Introduction   1

Chapter 1

THE BACK STORY – FROM MUM TO BOSS   5

My early years   15
So what's your story?   19

Chapter 2

BECOMING A MUM   20

Preparing yourself for impending motherhood   20
Pregnancy and work   26
Maternity leave   28
Pregnancy and the confidence conundrum   31
Birth   40
Baby blues   43
For partners: when your other half is dealing
with PND or a traumatic birth   50
Second time around – moving on from a
traumatic birth   52
Be good to yourself   56

Chapter 3

CONFIDENCE, IMPOSTER SYNDROME AND RETURNING TO WORK 59

Your reasons for working 60
Kids can knock your confidence 64
Regain your self-belief and start small 67
Have the confidence to build an online business 72
Stop comparing 81
Seize opportunities 86
Returning to employment feeling confident 87
Imposter syndrome 99

Chapter 4

HOW TO HUSTLE – BUILDING A BUSINESS FROM YOUR PASSIONS 105

Being a mother-hustler 105
What to blog about 107
The standard work day doesn't suit parents 111
How to recognise when you are ready to pivot 115
Parents with portfolio careers 118
Finding your tribe and dealing with naysayers
and trolls 121
Keeping your fire burning 130
Boost your creativity 133

Chapter 5

MUM GUILT AND THE ART OF JUGGLING 136

How to prioritise 138
Letting go of the guilt 140
Decide what you want from work 142
Sharing the parenting load 144
Space to work from home 145
Childcare 149
Tips for happy juggling 150

Chapter 6
BLOGGING, VLOGGING AND BUILDING AN ONLINE BUSINESS 152

Vlogging for beginners 155
Create a personal brand 158
The recipe for online success 160
Know your worth and what to charge 164
Get rehired 167
Networking, on- and offline 169
Getting investors on board 172
Handling your accounts 172

Chapter 7
HOW TO BE YOUR OWN BEST PUBLICIST 178

My top PR tips 180
Creating a buzz around the bizz 186
Management 189
Get to know SEO 190
My favourite social media handles 199

Chapter 8
HAPPILY EVER AFTER? 201

Why it's worth it 205
The traps of success 207
And remember – don't get bogged down by
numbers 208

Acknowledgements 211
Index 215

INTRODUCTION

've been referred to as a #mumboss online for years, and I find it both a fitting and empowering tribute to the two spheres of my world that make me feel whole. I'm bossing it at work and at home, and you will be too once you've read my manifesto on merging family and work life. Motherhood, while hard at times, inspired me to be the boss of my life. A mumboss.

A mumboss is a woman who doesn't stop wanting to achieve her work goals just because kids have come along. She still has career aspirations, but needs to find a new way to work – a more flexible one that takes account of her family. Despite what she'd assumed, motherhood has fuelled her ambition: her kids have made her more creative, focused and business-minded than before (after the tumultuous, sleep-deprived first few months or years, of course). Who would have thought it? Not her. Nobody told her.

In this book, I will be sharing my own story – from first-time pregnancy to losing, and later regaining, my identity and voice after a difficult birth, and going on to build a personal brand and a six-figure-plus online business. I started Honest Mum, my now critically acclaimed parenting and lifestyle blog (ooh la la) at my lowest ebb. I was broken when I first hit publish back in the day (2010). I was struggling with birth trauma, and was far from the person you see today – the woman smiling at you from the front cover of this book, looking like she has her shit together. Then, I was a shell of myself, lacking confidence, purpose and drive. If I could start what quickly became a thriving blogging and vlogging business, so can you.

I used the fewer hours I had to work smarter and with greater clarity (nothing like pressure to sharpen the mind), and became more committed to getting my work – and voice – out there into the world, changing my life and inspiring others in the process. Thanks to the internet, this mum now had an accessible, democratic and liberating platform in which to leave her mumboss mark. With just a laptop and my kitchen table, it was possible to build a successful business.

The best bit is that everything I've achieved is 100 per cent attainable and achievable to all. That's the beauty of this free-for-all internet we have in the Western world. Your potential business is in the palm of your hand already. No need for overheads, bank loans or fancy equipment. You've got a laptop and a kitchen table? Great, you're good to go. You've faced the toughest challenge of your life already, remember: pregnancy and having a newborn. You're made of tough stuff, girl. You've got this, I promise. Dreams are so often sacrificed or put on hold indefinitely when kids come along, but that no longer needs to be the case if you want, or need, to work. The rise in the number of parenting bloggers is testament to that.

Having a baby can shatter your identity and your confidence. In this book I show you how to regain your self-belief and rediscover who you are, and how being *you* is your unique selling point when you share it with the world. Use your time away from the workplace to reassess your work life, and find out how blogging and vlogging can be either simply a creative outlet for you, or a new business model. Here you will find everything you need to know to create a business of your own, or to return to work with clarity and confidence. And for those doing the toughest job of all, being a stay-at-home mum, it will also appeal, because it can help you to create a hobby you might decide to monetise one day. Choosing or needing to stay at home to raise a family is a wonderful gift to your kids. Creating a blog or platform for fun or money can provide you with much-needed 'you time' and enriching opportunities for all the family.

I'll be covering the importance of integrity and being yourself on- and offline, as well as sharing my expertise on the written word and filmmaking (digital storytelling). I will also give you my best tips on marketing and PR to help you harness both the visibility and dollar you deserve.

You'll find many a pearl of wisdom from fellow mumbosses (and fathers) throughout the book, too – parents who walked the walk, talked the talk and got (or even made) the T-shirt – in the hope you'll feel less alone and better prepared to seize the life you want. The skills I've honed as a mother have proved, and continue to prove, invaluable to my work, while my leadership skills at work help me to manage my home life. The now finely tuned repertoire of mama skills spans everything from, 'I can survive on broken sleep for months' to negotiating with the biggest of divas: my kids. Becoming my own boss was my personal solution to leaving my former job where I was working twelve-hour days on set as a director. I soon discovered that blogging and vlogging professionally was as fulfilling, creative and well paid as directing films and TV programmes and, vitally, it meant that I didn't have to miss out on time with my kids: my number one priority.

There are of course lots of dadbosses out there too, many of whom I've interviewed on my blog in my #Dadboss series, and some of whom also feature in this book: men who divide parental responsibility equally with their partners, those who work freelance or part time, or who became stay-at-home dads. This book will appeal to all parents – mums and dads – but in light of the inequalities of the workforce for women in particular, its priority is to inform, empower and mobilise mothers.

Both roles, mum and boss, are inextricably linked for me; one simply cannot exist without the other. Furthermore, had I not become a mum, I would not have started my blog honestmum. com and organically become a boss. It was impossible to predict the power of the internet, or the growth of tech, when I started my blog. Equally, it was unimaginable for me at that time to think that motherhood would become the gateway to career success and financial security. I underwent a complete 360, from being predominantly behind the camera, to firmly in front and public facing, with a global online magazine to call my own. I work hard and I love what I do.

I now live and breathe the mumboss way of life and want to offer you the confidence to do so too. I want to prepare you for the highs, the lows, the guilt and the joy, informing and inspiring you, so, like me, you too can survive and thrive at work and at home. I thought kids would hinder my career before I became a mumboss. I couldn't have been more wrong.

Chapter 1

THE BACK STORY –
FROM MUM TO BOSS

To give you a bit of context, let's start by looking at my early career, and how I became a mum and a blogger.

I'd always longed to be a mother. Despite being ambitious as a child, and then as a young woman, I was certain I would never sacrifice motherhood for my career. I was maternal from a young age, and children have always seemed drawn to me. They still are. I was nicknamed the 'Pied Piper' by my uni housemates during my MA – our student digs were on a street full of families and our mini-neighbours, aged between four and ten, were my biggest fans. I'd arrive home from a day of lectures to find an assembly line of kids waiting patiently outside my door, anxious to tell me about their day or their latest football trick.

I suppose I was viewed as a big sister to the kids on the block – someone they could vaguely relate to who gave them time and respect, listened to their stories and made them laugh. When I appeared in the local paper in connection with my MA graduation film, the young girl who lived next door proudly presented me with a scrapbook in which she'd carefully glued the cutting. Feeling I was her role model of sorts made me realise the responsibility I had as a budding filmmaker – as I do now, as a creative and mum of two.

Over the years, lots of weirdly wonderful moments with kids have occurred. I remember walking down a street in East London with a med-school friend of mine when a young girl we passed literally saw me, stopped and ran towards me with open arms. My pal, now a doctor, came to the 'medical' conclusion (*cough) that kids relate to me on account of my large features, deeming me a big baby myself! Others have similarly suggested that it's the 'Disney effect': big eyes and a warm smile which draw people in. I'm a huge Disney fan so that warms my heart. I actually think kids are perceptive and in tune with the energies of others. They react instinctively and are drawn to those who haven't let adulthood dampen their imagination and joie de vivre.

I later worked as a lecturer and teacher, educating and nurturing teens and tweens in socially deprived and affluent areas respectively. I was inspired by my students' determination and tenacity, particularly those experiencing grave challenges: the refugees and immigrants who, despite adversity, were determined to succeed. I was both teacher and confidant to those young adults, using tools to inform, but also to nurture and support.

Supporting others to reach their potential has been my life-long ambition; it's in my DNA, as I come from a long line of teachers and university lecturers. My mother lectured in sociology, politics and English literature, and her influence informs every post I write or video I make. I constantly ask myself when creating, how I can serve and help others? Nothing feels more rewarding than empowering people to make a difference.

I've always been creative. I've written, taught, directed, animated and painted for years. My mum has pictures of my many detailed drawings from the age of two, and a sparrowhawk I drew in pastel colours, aged six, was deemed so sophisticated by teachers that my parents were called in to view it. It's now duly framed in their downstairs toilet. I later exhibited oils in a prestigious pop-up Mayfair gallery for charity, aged sixteen (selling my piece too), and was one of – if not the first – to incorporate video art into my A-Level Art submission, which was regarded as ground-breaking at the time. It seems I've always liked to push boundaries, a sensibility born from a 'Why not?' attitude inherited from my tenacious father.

Art and expressing myself through oils, and later the moving image, has always been my saving grace. My creativity is a vehicle through which to understand and process the world around me, as well as my release from fear and stress.

When my first son, Oliver, was born, there was no longer space nor, indeed, any time for the arts in my new life. Those creative pursuits – which had always inspired, enlivened and soothed me – suddenly felt unobtainable and somewhat frivolous now that I was a mum with a baby who failed to sleep. On reflection, that lack of creativity in my life was, for me, one of the most soul-destroying aspects of first-time motherhood. It felt disorientating to no longer do what I loved – be it writing or filmmaking – and this only reinforced my fear that normality would never resume. Sheer loneliness, with no capacity for self-expression or creative therapy, affected me more than I realised at the time. I felt silenced.

Ten months later, I found the courage to start a blog. It quickly became an emotional lifeline. Not only was it a means to share my life with others, but more importantly, a way to connect with those who understood what I was going through: essentially a personality transplant. I was lost, alone, riddled with self-doubt and without many mum friends to call my own. Blogging provided for me in every way: it enabled me to flex my creativity, find my voice and tribe, and cultivate a completely new career – a career I craved and wanted to succeed so that I could work but also spend as much time as possible with my baby.

The timing worked in my favour too. Blogs were becoming popular because mothers were not buying magazines, or tuning in to scheduled telly, as they had been pre-kids. Their babies, not the *Radio Times*, became their new schedulers. Holding a phone in one hand and a baby in the other made absolute sense to the blog reader – and later, blogger. Plus, standard telly didn't appeal as much to the new mother. An avid follower of the news pre-child, I found I could no longer handle the trauma (even the Halloween Special of *The Simpsons* scared me): emotions run high once babies are born, as does fear. Loving so hard feels vulnerable. You created life and can't bear to lose it.

New parents want to read about and connect with other parents. They want answers to their questions, reassurance for their fears and entertainment. As they grow in strength and assurance, as their babies do too, many seek a flexible way to work and generate income. So it's no surprise that parents embrace blogs and social media in all its guises. I found solace first in American bloggers, who got there ahead of anyone else, before starting my own as a means to all of the above.

Freelance journalist and mum of two Linda Rodriguez McRobbie likens the birth of parenting blogs to the Tupperware tradition of the past:

'The entrepreneurial opportunities presented by the digital revolution and the kinds of communities that exist on the Internet now are just as liberating for women as Tupperware parties were in the 1950s and '60s, offering them a freedom and flexibility that traditional, 9–5 work can't. There are so many parallels between then and now, but the peer-to-peer element is perhaps one of the most relevant – this kind of thing wouldn't work without the kind of trust that's built up. But even beyond creating new opportunities and new markets for women and especially time-poor mums, the internet has meant that mothers like me can continue to work in our fields. I absolutely would not be a journalist if I didn't have the flexibility offered by the internet, by remote working, by being able to work around my children's schedules.'

Like me, Linda's interests have changed since kids: 'The kinds of stories I write, too, have changed – I couldn't be a beat reporter, working on assignments out on the streets, and still be able to keep our household running. But I can write long form, in-depth, heavily reported think pieces and because I can do that during school hours, or at night, I can squeeze it in.'

Thank goodness for the internet, providing us all with the tools to earn in a way we couldn't before. I didn't intend to monetise my blog (I didn't even know that was possible in 2010), but within a few weeks of publishing my first post on November 10th, I was approached by the forward-thinking Bradford College (my first ever advertiser), who requested I write about their new course. I was admittedly green to the process, so the college had to explain how a partnership like this would work (rather like a magazine, as it goes), and that's how I earned my first commission.

Six months later, my friend James Berger recommended me to an agency working with British Gas and it hired me to offer blogger coverage on a large-scale project. The job was an exciting first foray into a slick, sponsored campaign as I attended first a press day, and later the British Gas Urban Swim Festival in London, along with my toddler and friends. I distinctly remember thinking that the campaign didn't feel like traditional work (natural sponsored projects never do), and it offered me a taste of what life as a professional blogger could be like.

It was on that first press day, over lunch with Olympic swimmer Steve Parry, that I met one of my best blogging friends, brilliant screenwriter and blogger Uju Asika of London-based, must-read blog Babes About Town (babesabouttown.com). I've since nicknamed Uju my 'guru' thanks to her endless wisdom and grounding, emboldening advice throughout both of our mutual blogging journeys.

Uju is always the first to give me a reassuring call, or to send me an uplifting Maya Angelou quote to emphasise the importance of embracing who you are and what you have to offer others. She's always there for me when I need her. The true gift of blogging – above and beyond financial rewards, or even travelling the world – is the meaningful connections you will make: the sisters (and brothers) discovered through 140-character tweets and long lunch meet-ups on campaigns. That's the real gold, right there.

Other 'sparkle' showed up as accolades, garnered during my blogging journey. BritMums featured from the get-go: to my surprise, just four weeks after setting up Honest Mum, I became a finalist at the BritMums Brilliance in Blogging Awards, in the Fresh Voice Category. (At the time the awards were virtual. They are now part of the biggest blogging conference in the UK.)

Touchingly, six years later, I won their highest accolade of 'Best of the Best', which blew me away. It was that first nomination, however, that was the greatest turning point for me, both personally and professionally. That early nod (I didn't win) was the biggest catalyst in helping me regain my confidence so that I could return to directing commercials, and not long after make blogging my career.

Oliver was one when I returned to directing. I filmed three online fashion commercials, and later developed a TV series pilot for BBC Comedy in Manchester (my short film *Rifts* had been optioned then). I soon discovered, though, that I could earn more money blogging at home, where I could be close to my son, who needed me, and work to my own schedule. By the time my second son Alexander was born, my blog work had fully eclipsed my screenwriting and directing career, and in just a few years blogging and vlogging became my main source of income.

Fast forward seven years and I've worked with many UK- or European-based, and even global, brands in the parenting, lifestyle, fashion, food, travel and beauty sectors. My schedule sees me working on campaigns while producing my own bespoke editorial, and sharing my life and loves on the blog across mine and others' sites and social platforms.

In the UK – and quite possibly the world (although it's hard to qualify) – I was the first blogger to be signed as a digital ambassador to an airline. I've also worked as an ambassador for one of the biggest global hair brands. In 2014, I landed a modelling contract with a luxe baby bag company, which saw me feature in adverts in British *Vogue* twice, as well as in a catalogue and on posters in store.

From a business that was just me for many years, I now outsource work to my literary agent, video editors, publicist, stylist and designer. The brand has grown too big for me to continue going it alone, and it makes me feel proud of where Honest Mum is heading. Each person contributes to the business as a whole, enriching and elevating the brand. Teamwork makes the dream work, right!

My greatest joy is being on camera – it feels like home for me. I delight in the buzz of a TV studio and a bustling crew around me (it's what I know), and can credit regular vlogging and Facebook Lives with giving me the confidence to appear calm under pressure – aka sitting on a sofa with Piers Morgan on *Good Morning Britain*.

My love of writing has seen me move from screenwriting to a more factual and personal style, in line with blogging, and I've also written online for *Marie Claire* UK, *Red* magazine, *Good to Know*, *Grazia Daily*, *Woman* and the *Huffington Post*.

It's important to note that a lot of my success must be attributed to never limiting myself to a single niche. I decided early on to reflect all of my passions on the blog – from lived experience in an online diary format to recipes, fashion, travel, hair and beauty and, of course, tech and business.

Sharing *all* of me, and the many facets that make up a mumboss, led, in turn, to working with brands across all spheres on the blog – not just in the parenting lane – and representing mothers as the three-dimensional people that we are. You don't stop loving style because you made use of your uterus, for flip's sake. This should be a given, yet archaic notions of motherhood were prevalent prior to the blogging and social media boom – and often still are when it comes to some traditional media and TV. How often do you see women breastfeeding in your favourite soap for example? How frequently are mothers reflected as women outside of their procreational capabilities? Which magazines focus on mothers and their stories outside of baby rags? Where is the reality in national press on how multifaceted motherhood is: the joy along with the pain. Who consistently illustrates honestly how complicated and messy real life is? Reality was, and often still is, lacking, but blogging and vlogging cuts through the crap and *reflects and connects*. And thank f**k for that.

As well as sharing my world online, I'm dedicated to championing women (and men) on the blog with my 'Wonderful Women' series. Interviews feature the likes of doctors, lawyers and charity founders, as well as stars such as Anastacia, feature-film director Sharon Macguire, Spice Girl Emma Bunton, presenter and recording artist Alesha Dixon and singer Cerys Matthews MBE, to name but a few. Emulating back-page magazine interviews, I wanted to ask the same questions of every woman interviewed, to inspire my readers.

My online work has led to offline opportunities too. Together with my friend and collaborator Jessica Huie MBE, we host popular workshops titled 'Turning Passion into Pounds', having partnered first with *Stylist* magazine and now the British Library. These are dynamic panels of entrepreneurial women transparently sharing their personal and professional journeys, and motivating other women. The last annual event was broadcast live to entrepreneurs in business centres across eight African countries and trended on Twitter. It's nights like these – brimming with electric energy, as women openly discuss the ups and downs of entrepreneurial life – that help inspire me to continue.

All this sounds like a dream job, and it is, for the most part, but, as with anything, there are negatives to this industry too: trolls and naysayers, long hours (the internet never sleeps and sometimes nor will you) and many sacrifices made along the way. There are always compromises, but doing what you love makes it worthwhile.

I'll be sharing how I personally overcome adversity, self-sabotage and crushing criticism when they rear their ugly heads, so that you can overcome them too. Despite the downsides, I cannot imagine my life now had I not possessed the strength to hit the publish button back in 2010. From a single view to highs of 80,000 views a month, and strangers stopping me on the street, my success feels absurd but wonderful all the same. Don't let that overwhelm you, though. Everything I've achieved, you can too.

Every single journey begins with – fittingly – baby steps.

My first reader back in November 2010 was my own mother, who still reads my blog today, so please know that this is all you need to kick-start your blog and new life: one person who's got your back, who'll read your posts, support your business and keep you going until, before you know it, long-lost family friends in Australia have found you thanks to a single recipe, reuniting your family and reminding you of the impact one blog can make on those you love (and those you'll never know).

This book will help you follow your heart and strategise your new blog and business. It will also support you as you prepare to return to work after maternity leave or time away.

Quite simply, it will help you find yourself again.

With fertility comes fertile ground to grow a brand-new you and even a personal brand if you choose to. Equally, the power in producing a baby can (eventually) help you return to work with renewed vigour, or find the strength to start your own solo business.

Now, as a mum of two, I hope to encourage other folks to follow my lead, to recognise and trust in the possibilities that working again, especially working online, can bring. To know that in these glorious Google days we inhabit, for the first time ever as mums, we're no longer handed the short straw when it comes to careers after babies; that procreating doesn't have to mean the end of money-making. Thanks to digital jobs and the possibilities they've created for work–life balance, we can finally work in a stimulating, flexible way, around our families. Sounds good? Well, it is. It's more than good, it's 'badass game-changing' good, because in my eyes, blogging and vlogging is the best job in the world.

Who doesn't want to write about all the things that make them tick? To feel their voice is being heard and valued? To know that they can truly make a difference, be it by encouraging others to support charities, or by pursuing a way to work in their own time and on their own terms, when they might well feel bereft of options? For me, being a blogger means waking up in the morning and leaping out of bed excited about the creative challenges ahead: writing a book, sharing opinion posts, covering a charity campaign, taking part in style and beauty shoots, creating recipes, writing for other sites – or a mix of all of the above.

I'm the editor of my own personal lifestyle brand and – unlike my work before as a director that was reliant on gatekeepers and commissioners to get an airing – now, if I have the urge to write, I publish on a whim and instantly connect with others. The internet is a level playing field for us all. How empowering is that?

It means that you too can become a kick-ass mumboss, and the aim of this book is to help you achieve just that.

MY EARLY YEARS

My mum likes to tell me that I'm a born storyteller: I was drawing from the age of two and writing imaginative stories from six. I religiously kept diaries since childhood, only stopping when I went to university – a decision that was in direct correlation to my meeting cute American exchange students who played on the lacrosse team and, equally, my discovery of the joy of Jack Daniels and Coke. Good times.

I embarked on an old diary hunt when this book was commissioned, reflecting on my journey from writing a journal as a tween to my online diary at Honest Mum. In a cupboard at my folks' house, I discovered my many diaries piled up high – some with shiny leather covers and locks, others featuring Monet prints plastered with stickers of Kylie Minogue and Madonna.

The puberty years were the worst by far – the absolute pits, to be fair – as they are for most. A delicate, slim child until the age of ten, I morphed overnight into this chubby, frizzy-haired, overgrown kid with huge brows, and the first girl in my class to grow boobs and get her period.

Drama saved me. I threw myself into school theatre productions, losing myself in other characters, and using storytelling and performance as means to survive. Looking back, though, my dream was always to be in television, whether on it or behind the scenes: acting, presenting, documenting or directing. I caught the performance bug from my parents, particularly my dad – affectionately known as Papa G to my readers – a #stagedad to the core, who himself loves the camera to this day. My folks often cooked on telly – and sometimes still do – and I distinctly remember my first foray on camera aged eleven, when BBC Two's *Food & Drink* asked me to present a segment introducing my parents, who were cooking on the show.

The dream began.

You can imagine my devastation, then, when I tuned in on the night of the broadcast and discovered my piece to camera had ended up on the cutting room floor – cue floods of tears and great shame at school the next day after my school friends had waited (and waited) to see me in my presenting debut!

It was a great lesson in rejection, at least, and an impactful one. I believe a lot of my success has been down to the fact that disappointment has never gotten me down for long, never won. That experience inspired me to be in front of the camera, but also – importantly – behind it, so that I could be in control of whether I made the cut.

Thankfully, I grew out of those 'puppy fat' days at thirteen, which was also around the time my mother finally let me wax my brows (bye-bye, Carpet World samples). My badass, thinner-browed self was now ready for life, and a diva was born. Luckily, a decade later, when I actually directed my first professional film, I'd calmed down the diva within (a bit). Even in those early days, though, I was always about sharing who I was and what I felt passionate about. Vitally, I was concerned with creating emotion on screen, the most important way to connect, then and now.

It was clear that I had always been destined for a creative career, and, once I'd started, I pushed on in earnest. At twenty-two, I gained a distinction in my MA from Goldsmiths, University of London after writing and directing my debut short film *Rifts* (the story of warring Cypriot kebab shop owners in

London). Channel 4 named me as 'one to watch' and 'a future creative hero', and I also received accolades from film festivals worldwide, along with a peace prize for filmmaking.

A career as a director followed – mostly social documentaries for TV and some online commercials. I also made the award-winning short film *Broken*, set in the 1960s, which still sometimes pops up on the box. Truth be told, I'd planned to direct my first feature film by now, but life had other ideas, and so did technology . . .

Having a baby at twenty-eight was unheard of in the world of TV, at least when you're in the tiny sector of female directors, but I had it all mapped out. Procreating was going to be a walk in the park when I was used to twelve-hour days on set. The movies had informed me that labour was a 'few shouts and it's out' – so I assumed it would quickly be time to take that cute mini-me back home, dressed in a sailor suit and hat, and get life right back on track.

Naive? Yes. Eternally optimistic? Definitely. Stupid? Absolutely.

One traumatic birth/C-section later, my confidence was knocked and my identity shattered. It's safe to say that having a baby completely changed me – as it does everyone. While I loved that Bambi-eyed baby boy of mine, I felt utterly broken, lonely and alone. I'd lost my bearings and nothing felt the same. By the time Oliver had turned ten months old I felt directionless and, worse (whispering), a bit bored. It's so important to be honest that parts of raising a baby can feel monotonous and boring. Babies aren't meant to entertain. Their job is to eat, sleep and pooh. That's life for them for most of year one – and it's usually made far worse by the fact that post-natal hormones are such a bitch.

I remember, just a few weeks after Oliver was born, pondering what to do with my time – with my creativity. I yearned for a space, a creative outlet just for me, during maternity leave. I needed to rediscover myself and my voice. So, I hit publish on my blog at honestmum.com, crossed my fingers and hoped for a reader or two (thanks Mum and Dad). Little did I know then that Honest Mum would grow into such a creative outlet and emotional lifeline. Suddenly, in just days, Twitter, and my site, had opened me up to hundreds of other women who felt exactly as I did. Teachers, writers, lawyers, stay-at-home mums, women from all walks of life – all navigating motherhood, mostly up shit creek, and all in need of someone to listen to them, and virtual shoulders to lean, laugh and cry on.

It takes a village to raise a baby and, in my case, with my first baby, it was a Twitter village. Just because those connections were online didn't make them any less real. If anything, it was easier to connect with 'strangers' and be myself, than mums I felt awkward with at baby groups.

I'd never shared with my husband or parents how difficult things seemed. I'd felt that to do so would be to admit I was failing – that it might mean that I didn't love my son. And while my husband was my best friend in the world, and was there for me no matter what, starting a blog meant that, for the first time in a long time, I had a tribe of women right behind me, who understood exactly what I was going through, physically and emotionally at that moment in time: people to chat to online at crazy o'clock as I breastfed my boy. Women to discuss careers and motherhood, goals and roles with. Women, and later, men, who simply 'got me' – and I, them.

Soon after setting up my site, my husband Peter and I packed up in Bristol, where we'd moved to from the Big Smoke, and relocated back to Leeds to be closer to my folks. It was time to heal, and to work in a way I'd never dreamed possible pre-baby. Everything had changed, yet felt like home. Because it was home.

My blog changed my career and my life.

SO WHAT'S YOUR STORY?

You don't have to be an outgoing extrovert like me to succeed: the beauty of the internet is that there's literally room for everyone – for you are your own superpower and organic SEO (search engine optimisation) means that a like-minded audience, however big or small, will always discover you and resonate with what you have to say. You don't have to be on camera if you don't want to be either; this is your platform to create the work you want to share with others.

It's easier than ever to build and manage a blog or vlog, with how-tos available online and digital support offered for a fair price, if you were to invest. I wasn't a tech expert on day one, and I'm not even sure I could call myself one now, seven years later, but my blog has evolved dramatically. I have taught myself to write code and I've not stopped learning, be it on the creative or the technical sides of being a digital storyteller.

I've consistently pushed to grasp as much info as possible – knowledge is power – all while writing and vlogging prolifically. Whatever knocks I've received (and believe me, there have been many, despite what may seem like ongoing success), I've always gotten right back up again and blogged. And vlogged. And again, and again. And so shall you.

It's really never been easier to show the world exactly who you are – to consistently show up with integrity and passion, and to touch and transform your friends, peers and quite possibly the world. Now's the time, folks, let's go!

Chapter 2

BECOMING A MUM

This chapter covers the highs and lows of expecting and having a baby, and how it affects your work life. Pregnancy and parenthood don't have to kill your day job or your entrepreneurial dreams. You might find that motherhood does quite the opposite, in fact, as kids served to inspire and mobilise me to start a completely new career ... after the initial shock and trauma of course. This chapter will help prepare you for the unimaginable: your new chaotic, but fulfilling, life.

PREPARING YOURSELF FOR IMPENDING MOTHERHOOD

Admittedly, this heading is pretty deceptive, as no one can truly prepare for first-time motherhood. I don't even think you can prepare for second- or even third-time motherhood, to be honest. It doesn't seem to matter how many babies you've birthed – each new pregnancy and baby can and will invariably throw a great nine-pound curveball at you.

You might spend your entire pregnancy worrying that you'll have a tough time once baby arrives, only to find that the easiest baby since CBeebies' *Baby Jake* (the kid *never* cries) has just been gifted to you. You might have had an easy-as-pie pregnancy that simply flew by, followed by a difficult birth and a bambino who wails with colic for six weeks straight, just like my firstborn did. Happy days.

No one knows what's in store once the bun comes out of the oven. Little people are loose cannons, which means that nothing, literally nothing, about parenthood is predictable. The smartest thing to do is read lots of honest blogs (I can recommend a few cracking ones, wink), be as open-minded as possible, aka 'hoping for the best and preparing for the worst', and sleep as much as you can (please) before you pop. I still miss sleep and my kids are eight and five.

Please also know that when it comes to first-time motherhood, every pending parent seeks out the positives and holds onto them for dear life, kidding ourselves in the process, not stopping to think that we could find ourselves vomming for nine months straight while pregnant, or that we might suffer with birth complications, a baby who doesn't sleep or even post-natal depression. We rely on that much-needed spirit of good will – that all will work out in the end – to keep us procreating. Granted, we are also a tiny bit deluded.

We recoil at screaming babies, tantrumming toddlers and oh-so-sulky teenagers, telling ourselves the little white lie on which the world's entire future population depends: 'Our kids won't be like that'. We believe it, resolutely, until we have (sometimes) annoyingly shitty, but oh-so-cute, babies of our own. Every one of us is that judgemental idiot pre-parenthood, and babies are basically karma saying 'F**k you, this is life: it's gory and relentless, but flipping wondrous and life-changing' so embrace it all. Life is messy, and nothing is messier than a newborn, whose sole job is to get messy and mess up your life (while enhancing it to the hilt) as your hormones cause havoc and might well make you feel like you're going ballistically bananas. A newborn is a shock to the system in every way.

Matt Coyne, bestselling author of *Dummy: The Comedy and Chaos of Real-Life Parenting*, accurately sums it up:

> 'Prepare for your new arrival by emptying your bank account, smearing vomit on your shoulders and yellow shit under your fingernails, and avoiding sleep until you think you might die' ... But if I had to offer any other advice I'd say, enjoy it. Having a kid is like having a hand grenade tossed into your life but it is life-affirming and funny and nuts and the single greatest and most important thing you will ever do. So, don't f**k it up.'

Embarrassingly, I thought that my first baby would be like some kind of cute accessory, a gorgeous addition to my life – a bit like my Mulberry Bayswater handbag. I'm actually cringing as I write that, but I had no idea of the work that went into a) being pregnant, b) giving birth and c) raising a human being. WTAF? I laid out my yet-to-be-born baby's clothes and imagined life would be a *Friends*-style stream of meet-ups in local coffee shops with like-minded mums (who were ideally on maternity leave from working in the media, so we had *lots* to talk about), and that the baby, once born, would slot right into my busy life on set as a director. No problemo.

I also anticipated that my kid would offer me 24/7 entertainment – a bit like when we first got a satellite dish on the top of our house or when my brother Solos and I had watched Michael Jackson live in Roundhay Park in 1992 as kids. Now that was entertainment. I was sure my baby would match MJ, how could he not? If you hadn't realised it yet, I was a complete and utter dingbat.

Let me state again for clarity, *nobody* warned me there would be a ton of boring bits, as well as all the amazing bits, to raising a baby* – not *once*. So, fellow parent, please don't feel wracked with guilt if the *major* snooze factor kicks in (usually on day three of no sleep when you realise babies are not mini MJs and life feels a little like *Groundhog Day* most days).

The truth is, as one of the first parenting bloggers in the UK, I found very few people were telling it like it is when it came to raising babies. In fact, very few people were telling it like it is *in real life*, never mind online. I had little access to other parents sharing the tougher bits of parenthood that I desperately needed to hear in order to feel *normal*.

I spent most of my first year of motherhood wondering if I was the only person in the world to feel like I was failing at my new gig, that I was underqualified and couldn't measure up to all the other mums. I felt incompetent, tired, ungrateful, lost and palpably lonely (like Carrie in *Sex and the City* at her book launch party, a series I watched on repeat in those oh-so-lonely times). Carrie and I could at least wallow together (she infinitely more glamorously than me, as I sat in bed, breasts leaking, my mind not my own).

Thank goodness for the many blogs, vlogs and social media channels in existence now, which serve to normalise parenting and all the crap that comes with it. Yet – a big *yet* – despite all of this 'nobody-told-me-how-hard-it-would-be' discourse, you mostly forget and overcome (with help) the heartrendingly bad bits (zombie-like fatigue, pain and hormonal dysfunction that feels like PMS times a thousand). And some crazy people, like me, plump to do it all again in a heartbeat – thanks to the

---

* They become infinitely more interesting when they start speaking, eating and dancing along to Justin Bieber. The first time they say 'Mama' after the far easier 'Dada' is pretty good fun too, and their contagious laughter will warm the coldest of cockles, for sure.

sweet smell of a baby's head, which is basically catnip for your ovaries.

Why? Love. That's why. It's the most powerful catalyst and raison d'être of all. That deep love for your offspring, that magical, unconditional, transformative, addictive love you feel for your kid (even if not instantly, because mostly you'll just feel *shock*), makes it *all* (even the aching vagina/tummy cut) worthwhile. Despite the many, *many* immensely hard parts to making babies (not that bit), big, bountiful, all-consuming love prevails in the end – even if you feel like you're drowning to start with. Love saves the day. Always. However rocky the pregnancy, birth and start of life with a new baby can be, without question it is the making of us all. Literally.

Becoming a parent is the greatest challenge of our lives: raising the odds, upping our game and transforming life as we know it. That doesn't mean, of course, that if you struggled as a parent first-time around and were put off having more babies, you failed in any way. Hell no, the trauma of baby rearing can put people off for life, and furthermore I don't believe those who have kids in the first place have a magical key to enlightenment or should feel part of some sort of sacred 'I've used my womb' smug club. Never. I have zero time for 'smuggies', full stop.

Equally, if you've had a hard time conceiving or carrying a baby to full term and have suffered the tragedy of loss, it's understandable if you feel you don't want to try again (and many simply cannot).

In my case, I know from personal experience how frightening taking a punt on second-time motherhood is. It took starting my blog, undergoing regular therapy and making a cathartic film on the pregnancy liver condition ICP (intrahepatic cholestasis of pregnancy) that I suffered from, to finally find the strength to even discuss baby number two with my husband. I share more detail on this in the next chapter too #cliffhanger.

We did it though and we feel incredibly grateful to have two healthy, strong little boys, Oliver and Alexander. Was it easy to decide to have another baby after a traumatic birth? Nope. I write that, however, before admitting that I wouldn't rule out a third baby one day, if we are lucky enough, but I know it took creating a self-care kit to feel ready to go there again. I'm acutely aware that once you've hit rock bottom, the fear that it will happen again never really leaves you. That darkness. That fear lurking in the background, humming away like muzak, reminding you that you never want to feel so low again.

The purpose of this chapter (and book), however, is not to scare you with my honesty but to demystify the experience of motherhood for mums-to-be so that, when you're ready, this book will help inspire you to embrace a new way of life in fully enriching mumboss mode. I want to reassure you that having kids and running a business, or returning to work, really can be done.

I remember worrying that I'd be regarded as a freak by my health visitor and GP when I struggled emotionally after having my first child. I feared that admitting how I felt would mark me as an unfit mother and that my son would be taken away from me by social services. I know now that those anxieties were unfounded, but they felt like a real threat at the time. I was even warned by fellow mums to put on a brave face at my six-week check-up and not show any signs of weakness. I wish I could travel back in time to 2010 and give myself a big pep talk and hug. I'd tell myself to share, and that all would work out in the end.

Look, I don't want you to worry as I did, or to feel frightened and alone. Everyone takes time to find their parental groove and we're all winging it in full swing as we go. Let's embrace the chaos, but reach out for help when we need it, yeah!

Below I share my 'from pregnancy to mum of two' journey,

with tips on getting through the good and the not-so good bits. So, let's start at the beginning: being up the duff.

PREGNANCY AND WORK

You can't fully imagine how you'll feel or react, either physically or emotionally, to being with child. In the same way, you can't anticipate how your pregnancy will pan out, or be certain what sort of a birth you'll have (oh, the irony of the birth 'plan'). Birth like everything else in life is, frankly, left to fate and the temperamental MOFO, Mother Nature. Sometimes the sun shines, other times (mostly in Yorkshire), it pisses it down.

It's fair to say I took something of a risk with my career by having a baby at twenty-eight (I turned twenty-nine when he was born), so I empathise if you too are worried that you've set yourself back somewhat. We don't have an equal workforce, with the greatest issue being a lack of flexibility for working mums. This means that, unfairly, having kids poses a threat to career progression and employment stability.

The skills motherhood elicits (creativity, multitasking, prioritising, budgeting) are strengths that so many jobs require and rely upon, yet, frustratingly, a huge number of talented mothers are lost due to 'child-unfriendly' fields, where long, inflexible hours are the norm and career breaks are frowned upon. You tend to be in your mid- to late thirties by the time you find your stride in the media industry and enjoy relative commercial success, making it hard to ever find the right time to jump off the ladder and fit in child rearing. There never seems to be a 'right time' really.

The powerful force that overpowered my fear of losing my job was something I couldn't control or stall: my maternal instinct. My husband had been keen to have kids two years before, but my own broodiness kicked in overnight when I was twenty-eight. I simply woke up one day and craved a baby.

Another reason I wanted to get on with having kids was the fertility time bomb ticking away inside me. Diagnosed with PCOS (polycystic ovary syndrome, one of the leading causes of infertility) aged nineteen, I was advised by my consultant to have babies before I turned thirty. I remember sitting in her clinic wondering how I would ever meet the person I'd want to settle down with before the age of thirty, and then have kids with them. As someone desperate to crack the film industry, I literally scoffed at the notion of having children that young. Surprisingly, I met my now-husband, Peter, at twenty-four, and four years later we were lucky to conceive quickly and without intervention.

Filmmaking as a career, I discovered for myself, was pretty incompatible with raising a young family. Spending twelve hours on set just wasn't feasible long term with a baby, and as directing gigs can come up anywhere in the country, it pained me to be away from my child, who needed me, and I, him. I worked away from Oliver for two weeks directing online commercials when he turned one, and it broke my heart. I literally ached being apart from him. It felt unnatural. A few days away from my kids, even now, is tough going, let alone when Oliver was a baby. It's as if your heart operates outside of yourself, beating in another city, as you roam around like a head/heart-less chicken, disconnected from your whole self.

I was, however, self-employed pre-kids, so I needed to get back on set to help pay the bills – and to get back in the saddle before forgetting how to ride, and before the industry forgot me too. As a freelancer, I knew my career prospects post-baby were unstable, so I had started to save money throughout my pregnancy and I worked for the majority of it. That way, I had some financial stability, along with the maternity allowance I was eligible for (which wasn't much). Being a teacher and university lecturer meant that I had a back-up plan and could rejoin teacher agencies, and hopefully gain employment if I needed to, which gave me peace of mind.

My advice, either way, is to write out a plan of action and plot when you are planning on returning to work, listing ways you could build a secondary career (a shop on Etsy, for example) on weekends or nights that could take over your current job when it develops. That's the pattern most mumbosses follow. Continue with 'A' job, which pays the bills and offers stability, while taking a part-time course/working on a business that works towards 'B' job – the one that will eventually allow 'A' job to fall by the wayside.

If you're employed and want to return in a more flexible role, discuss this with management and HR. Some businesses (but not enough) champion flexible working practices, offering job shares and early start and end times as the norm. I thought I felt ready to return to work early on as I missed the normality of being around colleagues and the ritual of my day. I craved structure. I loved my son dearly, but I missed a job I loved and I craved stimulation too. Many women I've spoken to say they felt the same as I did, yet didn't feel confident enough to say it out loud. Wanting to work does not diminish the love you have for your kids.

I hope this book helps the voiceless speak up.

MATERNITY LEAVE

If you're taking maternity leave as an employee, most companies tend to invite you for 'back to work' style days so you can become accustomed to work life and feel in the loop once again. It's good to stay in touch with colleagues throughout your maternity leave and to take your baby in once he/she arrives, as well as staying in touch via email while away, so that important work updates and notices don't go unmissed. Online communication is a vital way to bridge your two lives, work and home, so you don't feel disconnected on your return.

The fine print

Statutory Maternity Leave states that eligible employees can take up to fifty-two weeks maternity leave, with the first twenty-six weeks known as 'Ordinary Maternity Leave' and the last twenty-six weeks as 'Additional Maternity Leave'. The earliest that leave can be taken is eleven weeks before the expected week of childbirth, unless the baby is born early.

With my first son, I had thought I was ready to return early on, though in reality I wasn't prepared physically or emotionally. However, with my second son, I eased back into blogging and vlogging more quickly. I felt stronger sooner and was raring to go, thanks to a positive birth and family close by.

On the other hand, many mothers don't feel ready to return to work at the end of their allocated maternity leave, so listen to your body and mind, and work out a way to make yourself happy. If you feel you need longer, or are suffering from PTSD (post-traumatic stress disorder) or PND (post-natal depression), it's imperative to be honest with your employer as soon as possible, using doctor's notes for support. Communication is key.

Many of my friends and colleagues changed careers or started new businesses during or after maternity leave. Others chose to become stay-at-home mums, or returned to work part time or in a job-share role. There are huge inequalities within the workforce for parents, so be aware of that, and know that maternity leave can potentially provide an opportunity to switch things up, try something new and make a change when it comes to your career. Michelle Reeves, holistic life coach and habit strategist at MichelleReevesCoaching.com, did just that:

'After a successful career in the City, I found myself struggling after our daughter was born. I was an expat in China trying to cope with a difficult birth and a premature baby daughter. On the day I was diagnosed with PND my journey back to me began, thanks to therapy, self-acceptance and a business now which helps others.'

I started Honest Mum on maternity leave and kept it going, despite my return to directing. It simmered along before, two years on, becoming my main job. Online businesses can grow quickly, particularly in this digital age, but overnight success is, sadly, a myth – even if it can look like someone has just appeared from nowhere. Any successful business/personal brand is based on accumulated hard work and an investment of time and energy. Don't be afraid of hard graft. It's the key to success.

Work and work until you cannot be ignored.

First decipher your goals and how you can chug towards them, slowly but surely, pinpointing whether you can ask family and friends for help with childcare, or if you can work early in the morning or late at night once your kids sleep, as I still do.

Many mumbosses, like myself, simply followed our passions first, and the monetising naturally came later. Anna Lewis, creator of Sketchy Muma and author (annalewisillustration.co.uk) describes her business as a bit of a happy accident as she didn't set out to start a shop. Prior to having her daughter, a few of the children's books she had illustrated had been published. However, due to her own personal circumstances, she knew that she was going to be a full-time mum for quite a while with her daughter. As a creative release during maternity leave, she embarked on a few funny sketches about motherhood, which led to a thriving business.

'I am an illustrator and I wanted to draw a book for my daughter documenting the realities of first-time motherhood in a humorous and honest way. However, when my daughter was nine months old, my partner became very seriously ill and my work took on a deeper more poignant angle as we suddenly seemed very fragile. I started to post my pictures more regularly on social media and began to get quite a following. My main focus was then publishing and my book *Sketchy Muma: What it means to be a mother*. My Etsy shop evolved as I was flooded with requests for my illustrations, and I have now sold almost 3,000 prints.'

For many bloggers and business owners, channelling their own frustration or sadness, and, of course, deep love for their craft, led to finding an audience or fan base that was able to support and buy from them – be it prints, clothes or books. Equally, bloggers became trusted figures who opened doors for advertisers wanting to reach niche audiences. This, in turn, allowed the blogger and vlogger to turn their passion into their career.

Reflecting on my job as a director pre-motherhood, I was acutely aware that a baby would pose a threat to my job. I reasoned at the time, however, that if I were to reach the pinnacle of my filmmaking career – directing an Oscar-winning film – at the expense of having a child, the dream would not be worth having.

Children meant more to me than fast career progression, and accolades (yes, even Oscars) on my toilet wall. That doesn't mean I don't want to direct a movie one day – I do, now more than ever – but I simply trust the timing of my life, and I've won bigger accolades: those kids of mine.

PREGNANCY AND THE CONFIDENCE CONUNDRUM

What does it feel like to see the blue line on a pregnancy test? For me, it was a mix of elation, shock and disbelief, as it always is, even if you've been trying for ages. I had assumed pregnancy wouldn't happen naturally for me due to polycystic ovary syndrome – that when trying to conceive I would need IVF, and could expect a long, arduous road ahead for my husband and I.

To discover I was pregnant within a few months was a complete surprise. That initial joy, however, soon turned to crippling worry as I started to bleed two weeks later, at just six weeks pregnant. My GP told me to prepare myself for a miscarriage. Having an early scan was one of the most emotional experiences of my life. I'd taken for granted that, now that I was pregnant, my baby was safe within me. I was young and healthy, so the possibility of a miscarriage hadn't even entered my mind, until then. The reality is that miscarriages are common, with one in four pregnancies devastatingly ending this way. I have friends of all ages who have suffered multiple miscarriages, and others who went on to have successful pregnancies.

Again, thanks to the blogging community, there are lots of frank and comforting posts from those who have suffered, offering insight, support and solace to fellow parents. Sarah Pylas of Grenglish blog (grenglish.co.uk) is one of those bloggers bravely sharing her experience to help others.

'I was ready to share my story in the hope that someone would find it when they were googling miscarriage symptoms in the middle of the night and would not feel as alone and afraid as I did. Nothing could have prepared me for the response I got. People started sharing their own stories with me and I realised many women go through this; I was not alone. Early miscarriage is not often talked about, perhaps because we are told it is taboo to announce a pregnancy before 12 weeks, but the loss is still devastating. Writing the post helped me to understand how I was feeling and publishing it helped me move on.'

Al Ferguson of The Dad Network (thedadnetwork.co.uk) vitally offered a father's perspective on miscarriage on his blog and social channels:

> 'The thing about miscarriage is that the story can change in a blink of an eye. Each time, I've been devastated, but the most recent time is different for me. I'm wondering if I have to accept that, for whatever reason, I'm not meant to have another baby. Maybe the world is trying to give me a message that it's time to give up?'

As my husband Peter and I sat waiting for our own verdict on the baby we so wanted, the sonographer said she thought, but wasn't certain, that the heart was beating, so asked us to return a week later. As the days passed, I took comfort in the fact that I was still feeling sick and prayed that my baby was growing. On our next scan, to our utter relief, we heard the thumping we'd yearned for. His heart was beating and he was flourishing, but this was just the first of many hurdles we would have to overcome throughout my tough first pregnancy.

Life did continue as normal for the most part, however. I simply had no choice but to get on with things. I carried on. I was directing a short drama series for a well-known production company at the time and battled on, despite puking my guts up several times a day, every day, from seven weeks on – which meant I had to tell my executive producer early on.

Legally, in the UK you don't have to inform your employer about your pregnancy and your intention to take maternity leave until fifteen weeks before your baby is due, regardless of where you work. Many women announce it to employers and friends at twelve weeks, at the end of the first trimester, as the risk of miscarriage is reduced and it becomes harder to hide a growing bump. I remember being thoroughly underwhelmed by my own lack of bump, however. My strong stomach muscles, due to 200 sit-ups a day pre-kids (Oh, how I laughed, writing this after two C-sections), coupled with horrendous vomiting meant that, frustratingly, I failed to look pregnant until I was around six and half months.

I was never offered a seat on the Tube and, despite buying tops to accentuate my bump, I spent most of my pregnancy feeling gutted at possessing the look of someone who'd simply had too big a lunch. Thankfully, my bump finally ballooned, and was picture-ready in time for my baby shower around the seventh-month mark. With it came the first of the many stretch marks I'd thus far happily avoided. At this point my sickness became more debilitating, and at thirty weeks I was diagnosed with ICP (intrahepatic cholestasis of pregnancy), a frightening pregnancy liver condition. I discovered that incessant vomiting can be a precursor to developing this baffling and frightening condition that, without management, can result in a stillbirth.

I seemed to have developed an aversion to every food I'd previously loved: meat, fish, garlic (crazy for this originally Greek girl) and fruit. I lived on cornflakes, the odd digestive biscuit and Dairylea cheese, when I could keep down any of the above. Clients were understanding (as they, legally, should be) and somehow, despite it all, I managed to direct and produce a social drama series of short films, featuring a famous cast. Despite the relentless vomiting, I felt more creative than ever. What a roller-coaster pregnancy was.

My friend and fellow blogger, the author and GP Dr Juliet McGrattan (drjulietmcgrattan.com), gives a medical overview on what happens to your body and mind during pregnancy (in case you don't believe me that your body goes through a heck of a lot).

'There's no doubt that having a baby changes you. Women are specifically designed for growing and giving birth to a child but it's a strange experience when your body changes so dramatically over such a short space of time. Many women embrace those changes but others struggle.

High levels of hormones such as oestrogen and progesterone trigger a cascade of events which not only steer the development of the baby but also ensure the woman's body can accommodate and nourish it. Blood volume increases by 50 per cent in the first three months alone, breast tissue enlarges and pelvic ligaments soften. Weight gain and fatigue are normal, varicose veins and piles are common issues and we all know how swinging hormonal levels can affect mood.'

It's funny when I look back now on how I thought pregnancy would pan out. As a somewhat impressionable twenty-eight-year-old, I'd imagined I was going to be a Victoria Beckham-style mum-to-be (forget that I'd never been her size pre-kids – details, smeetails). I was going to look and feel amazing up the duff, donning tight vests to show off my bump like Victoria, before strutting out of hospital as she had, in skinny jeans and sky-scraper heels, already sans baby weight. Bliss.

Now, for some, that's exactly what happens. And by some, I mean Victoria Beckham and approximately three other women in the world, including one of my best friends, Carlie, who naturally lost weight within days after having twins. (So not fair.) The rest of us find that our bodies (not forgetting our minds) change irrevocably once we've grown a baby. Nine months on, nine months off – cough, I mean five years off, more like! My youngest is five and a half and I'm still waiting for my body to bounce back. Any day now, right? #Mumtumforever, over here!

Don't let that put you off, though. With baby-making comes, eventually, a greater appreciation of your body. Even if I struggled post-birth (and for a long time afterwards) with a body that

I didn't recognise as my own, in the end pregnancy empowered me. Yes, I have stretch marks, but I no longer care and wear my bikini with pride. You just try to stop me! I even started a movement, #proudinmybikini, in which many other women embraced their post-baby bodies, sharing their pictures on social media, empowering others in the process. It's a rebellious act of feminism to love your body just as it is, so do it.

That's not to say it was easy getting to this point. After having my first child, I vividly remember feeling so embarrassed by my three-stone weight gain that I tried to cancel meet-ups with local mums so I didn't have to leave the house. I would hide myself in black stretchy dresses and long cardigans, trying to obscure the many lumps and bumps that seemed to have taken over my body.

Pregnancy pressures exist and seem to mount by the day, but remind yourself how ridiculous they are: it's near impossible to control your pregnancy body (or your cravings, for that matter) and the length of time it will take to return to any kind of normality – whatever that even means.

And yes, it feels demoralising to inevitably put on weight in pregnancy, particularly once you have had your baby and find yourself with a flabby, enlarged body – hollow and loose with a baby-shaped hole in it – but that's the reality for most, so please don't feel ashamed about it. Take refuge in the sweet fact that you are *completely* normal: that putting on weight and feeling shit about it is to be expected, and that the pressure to be or feel anything other than the way you do, in your own individual body and experience, is big baloney, so don't let it define or hinder you.

Don't do what I did and try to get out of meeting with other mums who felt as crap as I did, when all I needed was tea, hugs and honest conversation. Don't forget that most of us lose our mojo after having kids. How could we not? Our body changes shape, look and feel (hi there, tiger tummy and thighs), but in time, acceptance wades in where self-loathing once lived, and, when you're ready, you can improve your fitness levels, strength and physique until you feel kick-ass again.

When my first son turned ten months old, I actually weighed less than I did pre-pregnancy as I'd re-educated myself about the importance of exercise, pushing myself to run regularly. With a new-found love of exercise, I discovered that running and power walking gave me the mental and physical release I needed. It also worked hand in hand with my therapy to heal me.

Body image is undoubtedly one more thing – along with the crazy hormones and horrendous sleep-deprivation – that can chip away at your confidence and, as in my case, isolate you even further, if you choose to hide away. Like everything challenging with motherhood, though, it's important to remember that how you look and feel at your lowest ebb is not forever. So, if you're reading this overcome with self-hatred, know that I've been there too, and that the shittiness will improve and it will pass, I promise.

Your baby will eventually sleep (yay), your body will feel more like your own again, and in time life will reach a new normal – an even better normal than before, however unbelievable that might sound right now. Why? Because you'll feel stronger, more capable and even more attractive than you did before your baby – and you'll appreciate your body for giving you the greatest gift in life.

When you're feeling down in the dumps, the last thing you want is to get sweaty, but it's the most important thing to do – even if it's a short walk or swim, or working out to an exercise DVD in your lounge. Exercise is a magical mood lifter and will give you an endorphin release that your mind will thank you for. While it will be low on your priority list, shove it up there once you're physically able to. Becoming more active has a knock-on effect on everything, giving you greater confidence, a calmer mind, weight loss and the determination to eat better and keep moving, regularly.

If you feel ready to think about fitness again (and do ask your own GP first), sports and exercise medicine consultant Dr Kay Brennan (privatehealthprofessionals.co.uk) offers her advice on how you can become fit and strong again:

'Returning to physical activity after a difficult pregnancy or birth can be daunting. You need to start at a low level and recognise that it will take time to build up your fitness, strength and overall body condition. There is no quick fix. For most new mums, their return to fitness will start with walking, building up the distance, speed and difficulty of terrain as you get fitter and have more endurance.'

Kay advises joining a local walking group for social support and finding new routes. She also recommends mat-based body-resistance exercise as a way to start re-engaging and reactivating your pelvic floor and core muscles. Kay also suggests seeking medical or physiotherapy advice before starting any exercise programme in the postpartum period, as it is important to start at the right time and appropriate level in your physical recovery.

One of my oldest, closest friends, Caroline Asquith of ShapeShifters (shapeshiftersleeds.com), loved exercising after her third baby so much that she was inspired to become a personal trainer – another example of how having kids can be the catalyst for a career change:

'Sitting at a desk for hours a day after maternity leave made me feel hemmed in. The part I still loved about my job was managing and teaching people, and getting excited when they had success. I really wanted to combine this with what I loved doing best – exercising! So, three weeks after a brutal

C-section with my third baby in three years, I started studying to become a Personal Trainer, specialising in post-natal training, helping other mums with their fitness regime.'

Your body underwent phenomenal change over nine months of carrying a baby, so it will take at least this time period again, if not longer, for your body to start to regain normality after the demands placed on it by pregnancy and birth. My advice is to go out for gentle walks at first – the fresh air and exercise will make you feel better able to handle the stress of motherhood – then build from there. One good friend I would always push myself to meet up with after my C-section was Ruth. Encouraging each other, we would gently walk around Richmond Park together. As we both got stronger, we found ourselves power walking, and before we knew it, pushing our prams up steep hills. Not bad going for two mums who'd had C-sections four months earlier.

Emotionally, focus on your strengths and start a 'kind to yourself' list, noting all the things you feel happy about, and grateful for, in your life. List the things you've achieved, big and small, so that you can reflect on the daily milestones you've ticked off, be it buying or making baby food so you're stocked up, or taking some time out just for you. That might be going for a wee uninterrupted, sending some emails, researching a new business idea, or anything that's provided you with stimulation, purpose and good vibes. I'm a bit of a stationery addict, so just stocking up on new notebooks makes me happy. Pop online or to your favourite store and splash out on some brand-new pens and pads to give you a boost to begin.

Life with babies is a whirlwind, so getting things down in black and white can help you process your day, making a positive difference to self-esteem. It reminds you of what you're actually doing at a time when everything can easily blur into one another.

Gratitude lists have proven to increase self-worth and happiness. Please try it, even if you take only five minutes at night to scribble something down. It will uplift you. You could even start a gratitude blog . . . now there's an idea!

BIRTH

If you are reading this, pregnant with your yet-to-be-born first baby, know that motherhood feels a bit like this: you go from pre-kids 'I own my life and time on planet Earth and will drool over Harvey Spectre in *Suits* without interruption every single night, weeing solo on a whim when I need to' to 'I've just landed on Mars without a map and can't even wee without strapping the baby to my chest as it nurses.' Nice. First time around, it's like a, 'this shit just got real' mad-as-a-hatter kind of time that hits you without warning. Second, and no doubt third time around, you're more ready for the carnage and the fact you will never go to the toilet alone again!

I often wondered why a midwife or nurse failed to pull me aside as we were leaving the hospital to tip me off that newborns will mess up our lives, or the first year at least. To be fair, no one would ever leave the hospital if they were warned about the realities of parenthood, would they?

From one day to the next, your entire world flips on its head, irrevocably changing forever as you go from safeguarding a bump to being responsible for another human being until they're eighteen years old (or thirty if you're a Greek mum). Miranda of *Sex and the City*'s words on how surreal it is to meet your baby nailed it: 'And just like that, Life comes in and things begin to change. It's weird. It's like suddenly there's a giraffe in the room. Hello.'

What I will state, though, and what keeps people procreating, no doubt, is that baby-induced oxytocin-ified buzz can feel addictive. So can receiving the greatest gift to your ego: your mini-me that you went and made *Blue Peter*-style. While many will fall head over heels in love with their baby at first sight, many, equally, won't feel that huge gush of love straight away, so don't worry if you don't.

Yes, there will be relief and joy that you have your baby safe and sound and in your arms, but it's also totally normal and natural to feel anxiety, pain, confusion and shock – mostly shock – often before love gets a real look in. That emotional cocktail can make it hard to enjoy the 'happy feels' at first. True love can be a slow grower too, but, whatever your birth story, the bond with your baby will bloom and blossom over time.

I was chatting to friends about first-time motherhood recently and we deduced that this slow-growing sort of love when it comes to parenthood feels like an unspeakably taboo subject. Yes, another one. Like you can't admit you didn't feel one hundred per cent elated on giving birth in case you might not be qualified for the 'job'. That sharing as much might mean having to hand your cervix in at your next smear test or something, hanging your head in shame for the rest of your days.

While I deeply loved my firstborn, Oliver, I also felt incredibly strange, particularly as I was induced due to ICP, resulting in an emergency C-section and traumatic birth. It's not easy to deal with, accept or even write about any kind of trauma – and birth trauma comes with a placenta-style side of guilt attached to it because motherhood is built up to be this hyperreal fairy tale: something to relish and enjoy and be grateful for (which it is), but when it tears you apart too (which it can), it can be scary and isolating, as if you've gone against the natural order of things and must be punished in some way. Fear, sadness and shock simply don't feature enough in the 'story of motherhood'. Can you remember when it was last covered on TV, for example? Yet, so often, those are the exact feelings you will experience when bringing a child into the world. The traumatic birth of Oliver, now eight, was so hard to deal with and eventually overcome that it took me five years to eventually blog about it. It is one of the most-read posts on my site, which helped many women reach out for professional help.

Birth trauma refers to damage of the tissues and organs of a newborn due to physical pressure or trauma during childbirth, and also encompasses the long-term emotional consequences.

I, like many other women experiencing pregnancy, birth and first-time motherhood, struggled with a loss of identity, as well as the emotional and physical pain that birth and, in my case, a crash C-section brought. Trauma can occur, whatever the birth, of course. It simply relates to the circumstances of birth.

The Royal College of Psychiatry estimates that between ten per cent and fifteen per cent of women in the UK will experience a mental health issue, either during pregnancy or within twelve months of their child's birth. While most people will have heard of post-natal depression (PND), this statistic also encompasses obsessive compulsive disorder (OCD), post-traumatic stress disorder (PTSD) and post-partum psychosis.

My subsequent birth with Alexander, my second son, was a tranquil elective C-section. After undergoing both those birthing experiences, I urge mums-to-be to do your research, speak to the pros, trust your body – and importantly your gut – and listen to those qualified. Never let your heart override the advice of medical professionals, whose job it is to keep you and your baby alive and well. Birth is birth, however your baby arrives in the world. Please remember that.

If you're suffering post-birth, reach out for help and don't delay in doing so. Depression has no prejudice and can affect all, from superstars like Adele to Harry Potter-style Muggle mums like us. Also, your birth might be a breeze. Some find it and motherhood a walk in the park, but you must seek help if and when you need it.

*

Having a baby can feel overwhelming. Dr Juliet McGrattan explains, 'There's the pressure of responsibility with new parents. Being in charge of a new-born baby can be a terrifying prospect for many women, especially those who are isolated and unsupported.'

The biggest fear is seeming insubstantial as a new parent, but please know that the majority of us will feel, and *are* weak, after childbirth and looking after a baby 24/7. It's a strength, not a weakness, to admit you need more support, time out, help from your GP and therapist or, in some cases, medication. I wish I'd known that myself when I hit rock bottom, so that I could have received the help I needed far quicker than I did. Emotionally, when you become a mother you gain a baby, but you also lose a part of yourself (the spontaneous part), and it takes time to get your head around that. It takes a while to return to yourself, and collectively we need to talk more about the downs as well as the ups when it comes to raising the future, so everyone feels more supported.

BABY BLUES

I vividly remember the day we were told we could take our baby home from the hospital. It was frankly alarming! Oliver was born in January and it was the first time in years since living in London that we'd seen snow. The flakes fell from the night I was in labour until the day we left the hospital four days later. It was like Narnia in West London and the city was unrecognisable. It felt like what is known as a 'pathetic fallacy', where the weather reflects the inner mood of the protagonist in a story – me. I no longer knew where or who I was when I left that hospital, and I was freezing to boot.

Truth be told, if I could have smuggled a nurse out with me in my baby bag to come and live and care for us all, I would have done. My husband and I could not comprehend having to leave the hospital on our own without the care and attention we'd been receiving from the front-of-line medical staff over the past few days in hospital. We were lucky, as nurses had helped me to breastfeed and bathe the baby. They'd been there to answer my endless questions and keep me well. I wasn't sure we could raise Oliver without them.

I realise how ridiculous this might sound now, yet so many parents I've chatted to since admitted they felt exactly the same way, questioning how the heck they could look after a baby without a manual or training course. Someone needs to make that manual how-to video on YouTube if they haven't already – it would go viral!

My mum, who was with us for support, kept telling me repeatedly that she'd forgotten everything she'd ever known about looking after babies. We were basically a bunch of clueless grown-ups trying to make sure the baby was OK, which he was, apart from the six weeks of excruciating colic he suffered, and the fact that he never seemed full, so was permanently latched onto one of my breasts. I thought I'd leave the hospital with a baby that would sleep, feel full and be happy, not my poor boy who was screeching and in constant pain.

That, coupled with post-natal anxiety and trauma, was not pretty. Those days felt heavy and dark. The light peeked in at times, when Oliver looked at me and smiled with his kind, almond-shaped eyes full of love and, later, laughed, but most of my time was spent in survival mode as I simply tried to get through each day, with no real end to the unhappiness in sight. Physical turning points, however, came more quickly than emotional ones, and seemed to arrive in threes: slight normality returning three days post-op, again at three weeks, and then at six, when I was allowed to drive again.

The weird thing was, everywhere I looked, every other mother I saw seemed like she was nailing motherhood. Selective exposure, perhaps, or 'brave faces' all round. The chatter amongst fellow mums revolved around getting baby to sleep through the night, which is understandable when no one is sleeping, but it all felt overbearing to me – a pressured, toxic environment of mums who were thrown together based on a postcode and NCT class, and who didn't all naturally gel. I missed my old life, my old self and my old mates; everything seemed so laborious and hard. When you feel crap, the last thing you want to do is force yourself out to meet other mums you hardly know and can't be your monstrous self with (!), feeling you have to put on an act with the last remaining sliver of energy you have left after not sleeping for weeks. Some of the women I randomly met at baby groups were polar opposites to me, but I did meet some like-minded women and I hung onto them for dear life. Despite how tough it is to get out, go find your tribe – it is out there and the women in it need friends too.

My closest friends at the time were single and ready to mingle, having babies the furthest thing from their minds. Being the first of your friends to have a child can be incredibly lonely. While my child-free mates loved my baby, most, understandably, struggled with the new me. The mother me. Friendships changed. Accept this if it happens to you. Not everyone without babies will understand your new life, nor should they, in all fairness. I didn't have the foggiest idea about the reality of motherhood before bearing fruits from my womb either! The greatest life advice I've received to date has to be this infamous phrase from *Frozen* the movie: 'Let it go'. While some mates will go the distance, others were never meant to be forever friends. Thankfully I made some firm mummy friends, which helped, but the pressure of birth (because it's romanticised to a huge extent), and the promise of a magical experience that was never realised, served to fuel a cycle of guilt and self-hatred in me, making new friendships harder to form.

I wish I'd had access to stories similar to mine, to know what I do now, that I didn't fail as a mother because I'd had a C-section, that I experienced trauma because it was a scary time. I would have loved more practical help at the time too, but we were far from family, and while my husband was a dependable rock as always, it was moving closer to my mum and dad in Leeds which proved a game-changer for us all.

If you are worried you are suffering from a traumatic birth or depression, please know that you are not alone and will recover with help and in time. If you're unsure whether you might be depressed, this checklist from the NHS website should help.

Reasons for depression can include:

- a history of mental health problems, particularly depression, earlier in life
- a history of mental health problems during pregnancy
- having no close family or friends to support you
- a poor relationship with your partner
- recent stressful life events, such as a bereavement
- experiencing the 'baby blues'

And the symptoms of depression can include:

- a persistent feeling of sadness and low mood
- lack of enjoyment and loss of interest in the wider world
- lack of energy and feeling tired all the time
- trouble sleeping at night and feeling sleepy during the day
- difficulty bonding with your baby
- withdrawing from contact with other people
- problems concentrating and making decisions
- frightening thoughts – for example about hurting your baby

After relocating, I revealed to my family that I felt broken, and had for almost a year. As soon as I'd finally admitted this to my husband and parents, the support was overwhelming. I wish I'd had the strength to speak out sooner. I promptly booked an appointment with my GP and, seeing a locum at the time, explained how I felt. Frustratingly, as it took a lot of courage to arrange that visit, he brushed me off, stating that I looked fine and just needed more sleep (which I did), but I required more than that.

With the supportive boost of knowing my dad was outside waiting for me in the car, I persisted that I did, in fact, really need help. Again, he repeated that I looked fine. I was great at looking fine – I'd perfected the flipping art of 'looking fine' to Oscar-winning standards (let's call it 'brave face syndrome') – but I was far from it. Finding the strength to demand help at a time when I felt so low was one of the hardest parts of dealing with trauma, but it was the start of my recovery.

I left with a referral and a phone number to book a consultation with a therapist. Within a few weeks, I was given a slot with a nearby cognitive behavioural psychotherapist (thank goodness for the NHS), and the man who transformed the way I felt (along with my family, blog and the online community I'd discovered) was a hero named Toby Chelms. Despite the inevitably draining first session, a weight started to lift, just a tiny bit, signifying normality was in my grasp. I've since returned to Toby to help me through a less traumatic, but nonetheless hard time when a close relative was unwell. His work with me has enriched my life, but, importantly, shown me how to help myself.

The National Institute of Mental Health (NIMH) explains why new mothers might be more at risk of experiencing these mental health issues. They state that, after childbirth, the levels of hormones (oestrogen and progesterone) drop rapidly. This leads to chemical changes in the brain, which can result in mood swings. The fact that mums are often unable to rest and recover from birth leads to physical and emotional exhaustion that can contribute to the symptoms.

It's common, as it was with me, for parents to refrain from discussing their symptoms for fear of judgement but it's vital to do so. NIMH advise that, depending on the symptoms, support might best be offered by your GP, via your health visitor or through more specialised support, such as primary or secondary care mental health teams. You might have talking therapies, such as cognitive behavioural therapy (CBT) or counselling, or a conversation about appropriate medication. Nothing will be forced on you, but you'll discover what is available to you. Talking therapies could involve attending a group with others suffering from similar issues, which will serve to help inform and educate. It could also be on a one-to-one basis where you can assess patterns of negative thinking and how these affect you, or perhaps a chance to explore your own development and how this has contributed to your current situation.

My therapist Toby orchestrated an emotional first-aid kit for me, if you like. Now I acknowledge when things feel difficult, secure in the fact that I know they can and will improve, however bad I feel, as long as I'm proactive with self-care. With the help I received from Toby, subsequent dark periods have been shorter-lived and less frequent.

If anything here resonates with you, know that you can, with help, feel like yourself again, I promise.

To create your own self-aid kit:

1. Speak to someone – anyone – close to you, sharing exactly what you are going through. Don't filter, explain away or make excuses for how you are feeling. This is the first step to recovery.
2. Chat to your GP or health care professional and be clear that you need support. They will ascertain whether medication might be the best first option while you wait for a referral or

opportunity to speak to someone. You will feel as if a weight has been lifted from you when you speak candidly about your emotions. The worry I had was that I'd be seen as an unfit mother. You will not. You will be regarded as someone who has had the strength to ask for help so that you can recover.

3. Download apps like Headspace to start mindful exercises and commit to consistently eating well and exercising to help you feel stronger. I would punish myself by eating badly and felt that I didn't deserve to exercise, to feel good. Break the negative cycle and get the endorphins going with gentle activity.

4. Plan things to look forward to, but be kind to yourself. (See my self-care tips at the end of the chapter.) If you are not up for an activity, say so. People will understand.

5. Stay away from negativity – either people or situations that might prove upsetting.

6. Accept that recovery takes time, but you will get better.

7. Hobbies such as gardening and baking can help you to feel happier. Distracting activities gave me some solace.

8. Sleep. It's so hard to get the sleep you need to recover mentally, but lean on family, partners and babysitters to help you nap and sleep more.

9. Commit to attending therapy to break the pattern of negative thinking.

Susanne, blogger at Ghostwritermummy.co.uk, has seen positive results from cognitive behaviour therapy (CBT) too:

'After a traumatic birth, I started CBT counselling and am receiving treatment for PTSD; having the trauma of what happened being validated has been a huge awakening for me. Being able to write and to talk about what happened is the key for me being able to overcome what happened, so I intend to keep on doing exactly that.'

It was also thanks to my therapist Toby that I could contemplate becoming pregnant again. I'd learnt the power of working through issues, overcoming the sadness, and discovering and practising wellbeing rituals, while also knowing when I needed to reach out for support.

FOR PARTNERS: WHEN YOUR OTHER HALF IS DEALING WITH PND OR A TRAUMATIC BIRTH

Here John Adams, stay-at-home father and author of Dad Blog UK (dadbloguk.com), shares his tips on how partners can help Mum overcome a traumatic birth:

Practical help

- Spend time with your child, see what they react to, see what they like and don't like and get right in there and change nappies, help with feeds and so on. You will make mistakes along the way, everyone does, but don't doubt your own abilities, and don't ever tolerate being told that it's 'women's work' or that 'mother knows best'. I'm afraid as a father you will probably hear such sentiments. It's not a case of Mum knows best but practice makes perfect.
- Building on the above: you can help with feeds. If Mum is expressing milk or you are formula-feeding, nothing stops you from bottle-feeding your child and it is a wonderful experience. If you can help out with the 2am feed, all the better! If not bottle feeding, you can always wind the child and pick them up and put them back to bed before and afterwards.
- There is nothing like a good baby carrier. They are awesome and it's a great feeling carrying a child on your front.

Do, however, select a good one to ensure the child's hips are properly supported.

Emotional support tips

- You must never go above your partner's head or behind her back, but you shouldn't be afraid to express your opinion to medical professionals. If you know your other half didn't want a certain treatment or you have an opinion that you think is relevant, speak up. There may be times you have to be an advocate for Mum to ensure she gets the treatment she wants and deserves.

- Think about sleeping arrangements. Your partner needs to recover and rest. When our first child was born, she slept in a Moses basket in a spare room with me for the first few days and I bought her to my wife for feeds when necessary. This allowed Gill to get some much-needed sleep.

- Decide what's important and forget everything else. Your partner and children need your attention and are your priorities, especially if there is a physical trauma to recover from. The ironing isn't essential and neither is the dusting and vacuuming. I have a shock confession to make here: when my wife returned from hospital following the birth of our second child, we didn't have sheets on the bed for nine days! Slovenly, yes, but there was so much else to do that was more important!

I would also advise encouraging your partner to seek professional help if they need to. Equally, fathers can also suffer from PND, so again, do reach out for medical support if you are personally affected.

When keeping a tiny human alive, your own self-care can go

out of the window, so it's important to remember yourself. You need to be strong so that you can care for others. It's not selfish – it's necessary. Starting with food as nutrition is key to feeling well, mentally and physically. Small steps lead to big changes. When relatives visited and cooked for me, it inspired me to dump the convenient toasties and biscuits and opt for more nutritional choices. The move back home cemented this, with delicious, wholesome food on tap, supporting both my mental and physical wellbeing.

Laura Clark, BSc RD PgCert freelance registered dietitian and sports nutritionist (lecnutrition.co.uk), advises:

'Slower release energy-givers are vital – lack of sleep will make you crave carbs which is fine but make smart choices opting for slow-releasing, varied options. Magnesium helps with sleep (not that your baby knows this) so milk and wholegrains are good sources of this and keep your fluid intake up, especially if breastfeeding, taking water with you wherever you go.'

SECOND TIME AROUND – MOVING ON FROM A TRAUMATIC BIRTH

A tranquil birth after a traumatic one is, of course, possible. Sunshine after the storm. It happened to me after all.

I presumed one traumatic birth would result in another, but experienced the opposite with Alexander's. This wasn't a chance occurrence: I'd been committed to doing everything in my power to prevent a repeat of my first ordeal. Whilst I couldn't prevent my pregnancy liver condition from returning in my subsequent pregnancy, I requested the best care possible, and regular screening for it. Against the odds (a sixty to ninety per cent chance of it recurring), I didn't get it.

I was also much better at looking after myself the second time around, in both my pregnancy and aftercare. I also had a support network around me, and the fact my husband and I weren't first-time parents felt reassuring. We felt in control.

It is is entirely possible to have a happy C-section or natural VBAC (vaginal birth after a caesarean) following a tough, traumatic one. My consultant had advised limiting trauma by undergoing an elective caesarean, and thank goodness we did, as we discovered the umbilical cord had been wrapped around Alexander's neck.

Many women have successful VBACs, but my consultant didn't want the possibility of an emergency section to arise again. It was absolutely the right decision for me. I had a calm birth, and I'd do so again tomorrow! The surgical team was mostly wearing SpongeBob hats, Michael Jackson's 'You Are Not Alone' (how ironic) played in the theatre, and it was as perfect as an op could be. There was no rush. No panic. The anaesthetist held one hand, my husband the other.

The minute Alexander was handed to me, I fell in love. I left the theatre feeling on top of the world – almost as if I hadn't had a baby at all. (Those drugs are good.) What I did feel was *empowered*. In control. Content. Everything about the experience was different to my emergency section. I finally felt like I'd experienced the birth I'd hoped for.

Elective caesareans

For those who find themselves in the same position as I did, I share below how you can prepare for and recover from an elective C-section. I'm not a doctor so ask yours for more information, and simply use this as a guide.

1. Elective caesereans can still be worrying, especially if you've previously had an emergency one and don't know what to expect. The night before, I made sure I had a healthy, filling meal (I was advised to go nil-by-mouth from midnight the night before) so decided wholemeal spaghetti (slow releasing) with lots of lean mince bolognese (protein) and seasonal vegetables followed by fruit and yoghurt (eaten at about 11pm) was the way to go. I hoped it would keep me full until the surgery the next day ... and it did.

2. Keep yourself distracted and happy the night before. I watched my favourite programmes and comedy chat shows to keep me entertained. In bed, I read sections from comedy books, including *Little Britain* sketches and *The Royle Family* screenplays. Keep things light. I also kept calm with a large cup of chamomile tea. I slept through the night and my husband surprisingly had to wake me up the next day.

3. Once I arrived at hospital, I had a positive mental attitude. I told myself that today I was going to meet my baby. I had been asked to come in the previous week for a C-section and was then asked to go home and return at thirty-nine weeks (there had been an error when I was booked in). This time I was having my son and I was *ready*!

4. Just think: once you're prepped, it could be twenty minutes – forty max (probably) – in theatre, and you'll have your beautiful baby in your arms. That's no time at all. Keep that thought at the forefront of your mind.

5. You can usually communicate in theatre. The team is there to ensure that you and your baby are safe, but they also want to make you feel comfortable. If I felt pressure anywhere during the operation, I simply informed the anaesthetist, who modified the drugs I was being given. Being able to talk to him and my husband throughout was reassuring and helped normalise the experience.

6. Most doctors ask what music you would like in theatre – it keeps the op upbeat. You can also bring your own, so write your playlist before your C-section date!

7. Post-section, you will need time to recover. Mentally, I felt well and totally myself literally the second I was wheeled out of theatre, but physically even walking was a struggle at first. I'm not great with morphine and codeine, so I was only on paracetamol for pain relief post-op, but it was bearable.

8. Accept help when it is offered. Rest when you can. Sleep when the baby sleeps (and get off Facebook every now and then!). Ask your midwife for support when she visits, and speak to her or your GP if you want advice about you or your baby, or have any concerns. That's what they're there for. Eat well so you feel nourished and full. You need your energy.

9. Don't be hard on yourself (still working on this every day). Your tummy will take time to resemble what it was pre-baby and the likelihood is, it will never look the same. That's OK. You created life. Your womb did good. Give yourself a standing ovation (once you can, post-op of course). An incision has been made through five layers of skin, tissue and muscle, so your body will take much longer to heal than most non-C-section mums – try to remember that. Scars tend to be small and very low down, so if you want to rock a bikini in the future, you can. You need time and your doctor's approval before you can exercise. I was told to start slowly with power walks after seven weeks, progressing to jogging when my child turned four months. Everyone is different, but be sensible. You need to heal.

10. Never, ever feel you have failed if you needed, or chose, a C-section. You have done what was right for you, and all that matters is a safe mother and baby. Always. When you're ready, and can, have a day out to treat yourself and celebrate your birth experience. You are amazing.

BE GOOD TO YOURSELF

Everything comes down to self-care, be it during pregnancy, birth, at work or at home. You need to look after yourself and make that a priority. I want you to put yourself first, so relish these tips and practise them!

- Bath time is my favourite time. A relaxing bath during pregnancy to ease aches and pains away was bliss (just make sure it's not too hot), and when my babies turned toddlers, we started a ritual of taking baths together. Memorable bonding time for the family.
- Turn off the tech. Switching off the telly, computers and social media at least two hours before bedtime helps you to enjoy a deep sleep. The light from our devices has a higher concentration of blue light than natural light – and this inhibits the production of melatonin, the sleep hormone.
- Spring-clean your life. Step away from negative people. Unfollow people online who don't make you happy and work towards not worrying about what others think of you. This is made easier once kids come along, as your time and energy are limited and precious. Good vibes only please!
- Exercise, mild and moderate, releases endorphins and lifts your mood, however low you might feel.
- Get on the mat and practise yoga. With easy-to-replicate YouTube videos, the downward dog has never been simpler, and if you want to keep things low key, you can even practise yoga from your chair (following Yoga with Adriene's video on YouTube).
- Pamper yourself. I love to get my nails done and make-up is my armour. My mum recommended I put on red lipstick for my first outing with Oliver and it really gave me a confidence boost. Red lips and a lick of mascara help wake up your face – something you need with bambinos.

- Pop your PJs or coat on the radiator so that when you wear them, it warms you up.
- Keep a gratitude diary and make a note of all the things you're grateful for, daily. Experiencing and practising thankfulness and appreciation breeds positivity and boosts your sense of wellbeing.
- Play music that empowers you and brings you joy.
- Watch a movie when baby sleeps. Nothing can transport you across time, geography and space like the movies. Pure escapism.
- Read a book or magazine for some 'you time'.
- Nesting mode in pregnancy should continue once baby arrives. I loved sorting and streamlining. Now is a great time to simplify your life. Give anything you no longer want or need to charity, family or friends, and become organised.
- Practise positive affirmations. Remind yourself that you are a good enough mum and that, however hard life seems, problems will pass. My friend Ursula Tavender of Mumbelievable (mumbelievable.com) produces empowering cards that offer timely reminders of your worth.
- Visualise your dreams. Pre-baby goals don't have to die when your baby is born. If anything, new aspirations arise and evolve so remember that and nurture them.
- Arrange a night out with your friends when you're up to it. A laugh with great mates is worth its weight in gold. Date night is wonderful too: a chance to relish some adult time with your partner and remember who you both were pre-baby.
- Hug tightly. Hugging and laughter have been proven to help heal those who are unwell, anxious and depressed.
- Stargaze. There's nothing more humbling than looking out into the universe. The effect is calming too, and reminds us how big the world is.
- Create a baby book or physical diary. I adore ordering pics

online, cutting them out and noting down memories of life with my kids. It's so easy to forget those first blurry years, so this makes for a touching memento you will still read when your kids are older and, even better, they will read themselves.

- Remind yourself that you are worthy of what you seek. You deserve to be happy.

Chapter 3

CONFIDENCE, IMPOSTER SYNDROME AND RETURNING TO WORK

Confidence is the key to everything in life as my dad, George, would say. While you need to work hard to achieve results, a lack of confidence can result in others struggling to invest in you both emotionally and financially. If you appear to be unsure of yourself, others might fail to trust you. You need to believe in yourself to get the most out of life and from business too, so make confidence building a priority. Not confident you can become confident? This chapter will show you how.

To be lacking in confidence is like walking into a party head down, avoiding all eye contact and then wondering why no one wants to talk to you. Some might even confuse a confidence fail with arrogance when, in reality, you might feel the complete opposite: out of your depth, on show and full of self-doubt, making you appear cold and detached when in reality you want to connect with others.

Anxiety can change your personality. Because I've been there myself (and the self-doubt can be crippling), particularly after my firstborn, I'm proof that confidence can bounce back even when it goes missing in action for what feels like forever. Now, when I experience a lapse in confidence (usually hormone related) I trust it will find its way home again. If you're feeling this way at the moment, please believe that you'll be striding into that party (most probably a kid's party to be fair) with your head held high and a smile on your face before you know it.

The truth is, *everyone* suffers from self-doubt – they just don't openly admit to it.

As a creative, it's par for the course, as we seem to endlessly struggle with our own self-sabotaging voices, which seem determined to stop us in our tracks and prevent us from prospering. Then, of course, there are others who might try to pull you down – the drains, I call them. Some see you pushing yourself out of your comfort zone and, scared they're not strong enough to follow suit, will endeavour to break your spirit. When this happens, or your confidence wanes for whatever reason, stop and remember why you started your business or returned to work. Make a note of what drives you, discuss it with your partner, shout about it, but get it out. Find your driving force and let it keep you afloat through troubled waters as they arise.

YOUR REASONS FOR WORKING

There will no doubt be several reasons at play as to why you are pursuing your own biz or heading back to work. List them. Mine go like this:

1. I work to feel content. I'm in my element when I'm writing and filming, and I know that a happy parent equates to a happy child. Blogging and vlogging are a form of therapy for me.

2. I blog to provide for my children and to contribute equally with my husband.
3. I want to keep learning and growing through creative and business challenges.
4. I work to help others: my mission is to support my readers and viewers to feel more confident, as well as inspired and informed on how to start their own business, or to return to work, prepared and excited for the challenges ahead.
5. I want to use my influence for good, raising awareness on the work of charities, and setting an example to my kids and to others.

When I doubt my voice and what I have to offer, particularly in what can feel like an overcrowded online market, I remember why I'm sharing my life and view on the world, and who it is that I'm serving. That will be my readers, my family and myself. An affirmation that helps me is, 'I deserve a career I love'. I adore my job and believe and advocate that everyone should feel the same about theirs.

I literally have to remind myself not to turn on my phone the minute I get out of bed. Some nights I feel sad I have to sleep as it means missing out on writing. *That* is passion. Deep, all-consuming love for my craft and career. Once you have that, you have everything you need to build and flourish.

IMPORTANT MUMBOSS EQUATION
Passion + confidence + hard graft = success

Passion will always win over self-doubt. Don't dismiss that fact. However low you might feel, even the tiniest flicker of passion will prevail. The more you practise self-belief, the easier it becomes to believe in yourself and, by practising and feigning confidence, it will soon become your default mode, as it has for me. Can you imagine how freeing it feels to have a dream and to believe wholeheartedly that you can achieve it, or anything you set your mind to? It's the greatest gift you'll give yourself, and it's all within your reach.

Another boost I use to help provide self-confidence is based on the motivational posters at Facebook HQ which boldly ask, 'What would you do if you weren't afraid?'

Ask yourself, what would your brave and determined mum-boss alter ego do? She wouldn't let her own voice of doom or envious naysayers destroy her dreams, would she? Speak to yourself as you would to a close friend. You would respect your friend's goals and dreams, you'd encourage him/her to work at their action plan and put themselves out there, wouldn't you? You'd advise them to ignore the haters and crack on regardless? *Yes?* Now, do that for yourself. Take heed, too, of the advice of Tara Mohr, author of *Playing Big: Practical Wisdom for Women Who Want to Speak Up, Create and Lead*:

> 'Don't personalize the patriarchy. What I mean by that is that often, when women are feeling a lack of confidence post-kids, it's because they are buying into a certain story: I don't know what I'm doing. I'm a mom – not a professional. I'm a mom, not a leader/expert/executive.'

Tara says that this is a story fed to us to by a patriarchal culture that devalues motherhood and all that motherhood takes.

> 'You can change your story. The truth is, as a mom, you have become an efficiency expert. You understand prioritization like no one else. As a mom, you've developed more empathy, relationship, and communication skills. You've built stamina and unbelievable grit and strength. You've definitely learned how to get along with people very different than you (hello,

toddlers). You are now going to bring all this to mediocre boringness that is happening in most workplaces and you are going to blaze a trail and shake things up, in the best way.'

Penny Langton agrees:

'I went back to work after having both of my children and recently accepted a new role after the birth of my daughter who's nearly 3. I work as a marketing director for one of the largest privately owned house builders. Prior to having children my career and own sense of worth and purpose were almost solely defined by what I was achieving in the work place. Following having children, I became less selfish and acquired a more mature and empathetic approach to people and work–life balance.'

Motherhood forms the most incredible foundation for a fulfilling career, on- and offline, which can help you grow in confidence as you learn on the job.

Uju Asika, blogger at Babesabouttown.com, screenwriter and founder of collective mothersandshakers.net, started her blog to reconnect with her life before kids, while helping parents in the process:

'One of the best things I did for my confidence post-baby was starting a blog. Having relocated three times (New York–London–Lagos and back), my friends and family were spaced out around the globe. I loved being a mum but I missed my old life. I wondered: could I still go out to restaurants, movies and theatres, now that I had a baby? My blog and city guide answered that question.'

What is your question and how can your blog, channel or role at work answer it? If you're asking questions and needing answers, others will be too. Can you meet a need in the market and start something new? Can you share your perspective of the world to help others? Embrace your personality, insight and what you have to offer the online and real-life world and get cracking.

KIDS CAN KNOCK YOUR CONFIDENCE

First-time motherhood, subsequent pregnancies, a difficult birth, PND, time off work or a move away can all break your spirit a little bit and make you feel like you've lost your mojo. Having kids is a transitional time – a period of adaptation. That shift can be enlightening and life affirming, but it can also result in a lot of parents wandering around not using their potential, not feeling good enough.

Maternity leave, or any time away from the norm, offers you a chance you might not otherwise have had to press pause and re-evaluate your life. It's usually the first time you've had a break from your normal routine, a chance to come off the treadmill so you can breathe and decide what it is you might actually like to do next. It can be your chance at a second shot. Motherhood can be the catalyst for changing your career, going self-employed or returning to work on a more flexible or part-time basis.

Nikki Cochrane, co-founder of Digital Mums (digitalmums. com), a pioneering company that upskills mums with social media and digital know-how, explains why women often change jobs after kids:

'Whether it's down to maternal discrimination at work or a bid to find flexible working – or both – a lot of women become self-employed after having children. From our own business, we know this is the case with many of our graduates going on to find flexible work and the majority either setting up their own agencies or simply going freelance so they can find work that works around their families.

According to Citizens Advice, self-employment has become more female and more part-time with women pushing up the overall self-employment rate in the UK from 3.8m in 2008 to 4.5m in 2015. An IPSE report also highlights that between 2008 to 2016, the number of mums working as freelancers increased by 79 per cent to a total of 302,000 – 15 per cent of the total freelance population.

From our experience this is likely to be triggered by mums wanting or needing flexible roles to help with childcare, as well as new opportunities opening up for them to go it alone through, for example, the rise of online marketplace platforms such as Etsy and Notonthehighstreet – home to a large number of mum-powered businesses.

Whatever the triggers, self-employment is hugely attractive for mums wanting the flexibility sadly still lacking in most jobs. It's definitely not an easy option and what you gain in time with your children, you most likely lose in time to yourself, working evenings and breaks in the day to fit it all in. The benefits according to our army of Digital Mums, though, far outweigh any downsides.'

Parenthood can provide you with a window of opportunity, a chance to try something new, get out of a rut, switch paths and ultimately veer closer towards your dreams. That's what my friend Mel of successful food and family blog Le Coin De Mel (lecoindemel.com) did:

'Teaching has been my vocation for as long as I can remember. Before I became a mum, money was never tight. I could travel, save money, have hobbies, eat nice food and buy my first home. With 4 young children, childcare costs were considerably higher than my salary and I had to leave the classroom. Forging myself a new career as a blogger, recipe developer, presenter and photographer, with flexible hours tailored around my children's timetables, has taken time and effort, but it has certainly been life-changing and scary at times but ultimately empowering.'

It's frightening stuff going for life, and fear often protects and stops us from putting ourselves and our work out there, a risk that feels dangerous to our ego. It's natural to let fear hinder you, but you must fight it. It's weirdly comforting to lack confidence. It keeps you in your safe bubble, immobile. You need to pop it, though, and quickly.

Blogging was a gift I gave myself. Directing was never going to work for me as a new mother, but because sharing my life online evolved into a full-time career, I could still pursue a creative life – one that didn't require me to leave my house, or my young kids.

My friend, journalist and blogger Jacqui Paterson, had a similar experience to me. Jacqui launched a freelance writing career and later a blog, mummyslittlemonkey.com, when she became disillusioned with the traditional media industry. After leaving a glossy magazine job to launch a freelance writing career, she felt one of the big positives was being home based so she had more time with her children. With family in New Zealand, she knew the work–life balance would be a juggle, but within a few weeks of returning home with her eldest daughter, she was interviewing people on the phone while breastfeeding, and writing features up as her daughter slept in her lap. When the pressures of the traditional media no longer made sense to her, Jacqui decided to start a blog:

'By the time my youngest daughter had been born one year later, the magazine industry had changed completely. I just couldn't go back to the ruthless slog of finding and selling freelance features, so decided to use my maternity leave to turn my blogging into a paid profession.'

If your job isn't meaningful now that your life has changed, ponder your options and start planning an escape route utilising your skills and experience in a business or employment that serves your new way of life.

REGAIN YOUR SELF-BELIEF AND START SMALL

Regaining confidence, particularly after babies, can be a slow-burner. It takes time and commitment, but kids can change you for the better too (once you overcome the initial upheaval). Babies serve to inspire you and give you a new perspective, whether you're returning to work or starting an online business or blog. You might decide to do both: starting a blog in the evenings while juggling part- or full-time work. You might surprise yourself as to how quickly your side hustle grows.

You could write a post which goes viral overnight, securing you thousands of fans, or you could simply grow a small and incredibly loyal following (to you, and to brands), which steadily builds over time. Both can result in a paid career and both require consistent, quality content to retain interest and engagement. Once people start reacting to your blog posts, vlogs and products, and you make your first sale and blog commission, you'll feel encouraged to continue. 'Success breeds success, which in itself leads to greater confidence, rather like dominoes falling', as my friend, entrepreneur and PR, Jessica Huie MBE, would say.

Alternatively, perhaps your child is starting school and you've decided to launch a business you've been thinking about for a while. You feel off the grid and out of a routine – because you have been – so start small and slow. Tick off your to-do list and don't expect to be Karen Brady CBE on day one. Let your reasoning and passion lead you, and use it to answer your concerns as they arise. Remind yourself that you are blogging or returning to work because you love it. The challenges are worth overcoming because it stimulates and fulfils you.

I often feel I exist within two worlds. When my youngest, Alexander, was still at nursery even taking a day off with him meant a short readjustment period was required when I returned to work mode that night or the following morning. I know how hard it can be to straddle those two distinct spheres of your life, and I can imagine that four or more years of not working (doing the hardest job of all, raising children) and launching something new when your child starts school might well feel unsettling. That's normal. You can retrain your brain to switch into a different kind of work mode and, trust me, when you pursue something that makes your heart sing, everything will fit into place. With every fresh day, you see your old life merging into your new, and your business evolves. Yes, it's scary, but help is at hand to encourage you to make the leap.

Eve Poole, leadership guru and author of *Leadersmithing: Revealing the Trade Secrets of Leadership* (evepoole.com) shares that, unlike men, women won't apply for anything unless they are a ninety per cent match. She lives her life by *The Princess Diaries* mantra, however, that 'there are some things that are more important than fear' and urges you to do the same. She advises finding yourself first and figuring out what it is you think they could 'get' you on and ensure they can't! Eve's research is focused on maintaining performance under pressure, which you learn while under pressure.

Eve explains that you build the neurobiological templates to guide you when you are in a stressful situation: leadership muscle memory. She wants us to ask ourselves what scares us.

'Start scheduling in some practice so that you build up your resilience. Public speaking? Try giving a speech to thank those at a local gathering. Then scale up gradually. Ask a question in a public meeting; talk at a school assembly; and before long you'll be defending your neighbours on local radio. You don't need to be a master today, you just need to be working towards it. And remember, it wasn't the hare that won the race, it was the tortoise.'

The analogy of the hare and the tortoise is incredibly powerful. Everyone seems in such a hurry to reach the heady heights of success, often seeking out shortcuts over the long and hard game. Take your time, learn and grow, relishing what experience brings. Even the seemingly overnight successes have to produce consistently strong work to remain popular. Shortcuts simply do not exist.

Faking it – we're all at it!

When you're ready to launch, be it a blog or new business, or you plan on returning to work, believe me when I say that you can 100 per cent feign confidence until you actually feel it. It's vital to fake it, just as a method actor would a new role, immersing themselves deeply into a character's life and way of thinking, until they *become* that person. Basically, you need to appropriate Daniel Day Lewis. No pressure then!

Take a deep breath or five, smile and speak up. Don't forget, we all fake it at first so there's no need to feel fraudulent about it. Plus, nerves are necessary to give you the push you need to *act* and *do*. Yes, talent is required for success, but it's equally overrated. How many talented people don't use the gifts they were born with? I, for one, used to paint regularly and rarely pick up a brush now! Talent can be learned and honed through experience; the 'doing part', which has one snag: it requires you to start, and to continue. Try something new and commit to improving and growing.

IMPORTANT MUMBOSS EQUATION
(Feigned) confidence + action = experience and results

A word on results. The positive results keep you pushing on, the negative ones – the mistakes or failures – must do the same. Respect your failings for what they are: lessons. Learn from them, brush yourself down and *continue*. That's it. The winning formula to feeling confident and finding success. Confidence bags you the meetings, gets you the commissions and, most importantly, enables others to place their trust in you.

If you 'play' confident, then others will gravitate towards you and deem you worthy of the job in hand. When you present yourself confidently, people will choose to pay attention to your work (you need to keep them interested too, of course) and they will buy from you or back you. Perceived confidence (whether you actually feel it or not) encourages others to give you a chance, to take a punt on you, and a chance is what you need – a chance to be read, watched, hired and respected. When you are *confident*, you open the door to opportunity, garnering experience, learning and ultimately thriving.

Six keys to success

Baroness Margaret McDonagh was part of the New Labour leadership inner circle for the 1997 general election campaign and her six keys to success will inspire and strengthen you as you embark on your new journey.

1. Purpose

In order to have a successful life and career you need purpose. In politics they call it a cause. It is a purpose which keeps you going.

2. Resilience

No one has a perfect life or career – it is how you deal with those aspects day to day. Resilience is key.

3. Confidence

We often tell ourselves, 'When I'm confident I'll do x and y', yet it's doing the things you want to that makes you confident. We are more risk averse with girls and it's a real issue. Boys from a young age are encouraged to take risks and have adventures. The brain is plastic: when you worry a lot, you get good at it.

4. Networking

Women aren't good at networking and it's crucial to push yourself to do this. To work on team building. It's teams which achieve – never on your own. Sport stars still always thank the team that helped them become successful.

5. Spike

Successful people know the one thing they are good at and that gives them confidence. You need to stick in people's memories for those things.

6. Stop basing worth on others' opinions of you

Stop worrying about what other people think of you.

Yes , yes, yes! You are the only one preventing you from feeling your best and seizing opportunity. Take this important advice on board and start valuing yourself and what you have to offer.

HAVE THE CONFIDENCE TO BUILD AN ONLINE BUSINESS

My blog became a vehicle for confidence. It was the tool that helped me carve out a new identity, allowing me to reconnect with my creative self and others while doing something I always loved: writing and filmmaking. I believe that when you take the first steps to building something with intention and passion the universe meets you half way. You must trust that these digital times mean that a career in the media industry is now available to all.

If you want to blog but don't feel confident about writing, why not consider taking an online writing course? I would recommend you install the Grammarly plug-in so that you can check your grammar, punctuation and spelling (it works across everything you write digitally, from emails to blog posts and books). Don't forget that inspiration can be obtained from absolutely everywhere, so keep open minded, live life to the full and write what you would want to read yourself. That's the key to longevity. Trying to be someone you're not is exhausting.

Start, then learn and grow as you go along, confident in the belief that you can achieve anything you set your mind on, and work for. My friend Natasha Courtenay-Smith (of natashacourtenaysmith. com), bestselling author of *The Million Dollar Blog* and digital strategist, advocates a positive approach to learning:

'I generally believe I can be a brain surgeon and that the only reason I am not one is that I have chosen not to put my efforts into being one, but that basically a brain surgeon is just a normal person who has focused on learning that skill. So therefore, if we focus, we can all learn amazing skills that we didn't previously have.

When I wanted to learn new skills like video production,

editing and website design, I googled courses and paid £800 for part-time learning. I did a number of NVQ level 1s in various things – knowledge is power.'

While £800 might seem a lot for some, even a small investment, such as buying your domain name and paying a designer to ensure your site looks slick from the get-go, is a great start. Many bloggers and YouTubers use free online resources such as YouTube videos or the YouTube Creator Academy for all of their learning needs, from filming and presenting to editing. Equally, search online for resources or blog posts on blogging (my favourite is Problogger.com). Google your questions and learn on the job.

Blogging and vlogging are vital components of any business's PR strategy, so start there, even if your focus is a start-up over a blog or vlog. For example, your handmade clothes business needs a blog on your retail website and a personal voice on social media platforms in order to garner sales. Whatever your goal, you need PR and an online presence to thrive (more of that later).

It's easy and cheap to buy a WordPress template for a blog, or have a designer modify your theme or even create a bespoke site for you, and then to hit publish. If you're serious about your blog or business, *do* hire a designer (there are many at decent prices) and ensure that your site looks as professional as possible. Don't forget to have a logo made up, and the header on your blog should link to several pages that are dedicated to sharing your video content, your press, and your contact form, so you're easily reachable by readers, press and PRs. Do refer to other established sites like my own at honestmum.com and download my media kit on my Work With Me page (more on that to come), using them as examples to help you create your own.

When I started blogging, as one of the first UK parenting bloggers I don't remember there being a huge pressure to fit into any kind of mould – something that seems more apparent today. I suppose that's the joy of being part of a first movement of anything. Nonetheless, I've always held on to *doing me* irrespective of trends or what might appear to be 'cool'. I've taken an old-fashioned approach to a new tech world to keep my voice honest and authentic and I've worked my booty off.

Equally, I've ignored a view that one must conform in order to succeed. That's the antithesis to success as far as I'm concerned. You need to stand out to shine and, by being your own unique self, you will do just that. I'm exactly how I am online and off- (although my friends like to tell me I'm much funnier and naughtier in real life, so I need to work on that bit – I think gin helps), but on the whole, with me, what you see is what you get. Don't imitate: by being you, you're innovating. Trust your voice.

Being *you* is your USP

You only need to look at how diverse digital influencers are in order to see the power of the individual, and 'keeping it real' online. The bloggers and vloggers of 2010 and earlier were unequivocally themselves in a medium that felt fresh, unknown and pretty thrilling. Having a blog felt like 'our little secret' at the time, despite being in the public domain and 'out there'. For me, the magic of being able to share whatever is on my mind has never diminished, despite what should be a seven-year itch for me online! I get the same rush publishing content today as I did in the early days. Sometimes more so.

I bought a domain name and wrote my first post, 'My blog is born' on November 10th, 2010. I'd thought about it for a while beforehand, and then, one morning, suddenly made the leap. I reasoned that at any point I could delete my blog and move on with my life with the hope that no one would ever remember it. That was my safety net. Make it yours too, if it helps take the pressure off launching. I was shitting myself, truth be told, but did it anyway.

Fear shouldn't be feared either, as it goes. Close friend, renowned actress of *Brittas Empire* and *Ab Fab*, Harriet Thorpe's words on curbing fear always support me whenever I feel anxious about something new. Harriet also runs a vlog, What's Next Vlog, targeted at the over forty-fives to inspire and empower them (whatsnextvlog.com). Go absorb her wisdom:

'Work out why you're scared. Are you worried you'll fail? That's not necessarily the reality, it's just a fear. Your job, new venture is to be enjoyed and not to be frightened of. If feeling anxious, less than and negative, remind yourself that you deserve to enjoy the process. You might as well. Make that choice, you have the power!'

Let those words ring in your ear as you take the plunge to creating a new business, blog or social media handle you want to grow.

Feel fearless and channel your energy positively

Fear can hold us back, but it's about channelling that energy. As psychologist Toby Chelms once told me, fear and excitement are the same emotion. He explains:

'One common trigger for the start of anxiety is a misinterpretation of normal bodily sensations. For example, when we think about excitement and the symptoms that come with it (butterflies, a 'high' feeling, some minor trepidation) these are very similar to the start of panic. Therefore, if we are particularly busy, tired, ill or distracted it becomes very easy to think we are experiencing anxiety (and therefore, with a bit of fuzzy logic at hand, that there is a reason to be anxious). This is when panic can begin. We then end up feeling anxious about things we are actually excited about.'

Don't confuse fear with excitement!

Shola Kaye is a performer, entrepreneur and bestselling author of *How to be a DIVA at Public Speaking* – the step-by-step system to engage your audience and present with confidence. She is also the founder of Speak Up Like a DIVA (sholakaye.com). Here, she shares what helps her feel fearless:

> 'The key for me is to put my audiences first. Instead of think-ing about myself, I try to focus on them. Am I delivering value? Am I connecting with them? Am I treating them as individuals and having some banter or chit-chat to break the ice? The less I think about myself and the more I think about them, the easier it becomes. Be of service.'

When it comes to self-doubt, Shola likes to remember that the fact you care is a good sign. She advocates that you keep sharing yourself, putting the onus not only on what you know, but how people relate to you. 'Just put yourself out there – do your best work and let people choose you!'

Don't sidestep airtime or the chance to shine because you don't feel worth it. You are, but if you don't believe it for yourself, no one else will.

Once I'd faced my own fear of what it meant to start a blog, I quickly became immersed in the practical and creative side of the running of it. I got lost in the art of it, of teaching myself how to build and manage a WordPress site. I discovered, via trial and error, how best to communicate and promote my work, based on comments and views clocked on social media, WordPress and, later, Google Analytics.

As a screenwriter I was used to appropriating other characters, but had to adapt to sharing my own views directly, using myself as a mouthpiece. I essentially became the protagonist of my own digital narrative, the embodiment of my message; my life became my story. Once live, I started to receive comments, Facebook messages and even tweets: welcoming words from people who seemed genuinely interested in what I had to say, or those who related to my views and experiences. These people, valuable people, gave me the encouragement and confidence to continue writing, to go from one post to two, to twenty, to two hundred and more.

I'd written a few posts in drafts before launching, so I had several to space out through the weeks and would advise you to do the same, so you can pick up momentum with ease. Thanks to my supportive friends and family (the same people who still read my blog today), I felt motivated to keep sharing and, vitally, not stop.

Art is powerful and empowering. Over the following first year blogging, and thereafter, I regained my confidence. I transformed into the 'new Vicki' you see today. It takes a lot of hard work, tenacity and positivity to build confidence: to be rebirthed, if you like, after the birth of your own kids, but it's possible, and it's enriching and liberating and it's all there for the taking.

Collaboration as confidence booster

Collaboration is the most productive and fun way to boost confidence. Collaborating with other creatives is my favourite kind of 'work'. Two brains are always better than one so remain open to opportunities at all times. Be one hundred per cent ready for them when they arise or, my favourite, make them happen for yourself: your perfect business partner could be a parent on Pinterest, or a mum with her toddler in the playground.

That's what happened with Katie Massie-Taylor and Sarah Hesz, who met in a rainy playground two years ago, with newborns on their fronts and chaotic toddlers at their feet. They say it was a sleep-deprived and incoherent conversation between them that finished with an awkward swapping of numbers and, later, a thriving business.

Mumboss hook-ups are a thing, people!

Just a few months after their first meeting and becoming firm friends, Katie and Sarah realised their friendship had been a lifeline for them both in what would have otherwise been a very isolating time ... Eighty per cent of mums admit to feeling lonely as their lives undergo the huge change motherhood brings, and they are often by themselves at home for long days with small children. The solution was hatched and unveiled six months later: Mush (letsmush.com), a free app to find other mums nearby, with kids the same age and with similar interests.

Now, eighteen months on from launch, they have raised over £3 million in investment, have hundreds of thousands of mums using their app around the UK and Australia, and a growing team in their south-west London office. Their vision is that no mum does it alone, the world over.

If you can conceive it, you can do it. Having a business partner can boost your confidence and give you the strength to act on your ideas in a way that feels less risky than going solo. You are both facing the unknown together and can cushion the fear and potential falls (inevitable in all businesses) as a duo. Even if you don't have a formal partner, collaboration in my opinion is the key to success and, most importantly, happiness in business. I've come to believe that there are two types of people in life (and work): those who are only in it for themselves (mostly because of deep-seated insecurities) and those who want to collaborate with others and contribute to a bigger picture, helping people through sharing and supporting one another.

Some fear that collaboration might somehow divide, not multiply, their power, audience and return on investment, so they remain closed off, unable to merge ideas, share thoughts or make a difference on a grander scale. As a director, I worked with and led teams – sometimes in their hundreds – and, guess what, everything, absolutely *everything*, came down to collaboration, to relationships with others. All good was born from valuing each person on every single production, and working together as a team – without ego. It came from putting the film first and accepting that your best work happens when you join forces with others.

Furthermore, you must unequivocally trust that you are only as *strong* as the weakest member of your team, so pick your partners and staff wisely, and empower those who need to grow so they can give the job their best shot.

As a creative entrepreneur, I feel it is my duty to ensure that people feel emotionally safe, valued and able to *shine*; that they feel their ideas and questions are needed and important. You can see the culmination of everyone's passion, expertise and impact when you watch a film or video on YouTube. From script development to set design, performance, cinematography, the editing, music and more, filmmaking, in fact *anything* creative, is improved by collaboration – the meeting of minds. It's also how opportunities happen. Doors are opened (as people know people) and your end product will always be improved a million times over. That is why you – the way you behave with people, your tone, energy and perspective – matter. Good business relies on how you make others feel. Positivity and passion will always win the day. Those good vibes will get you the commissions, make others want to work with you and will provide the foundation for a content working life.

Ask yourself, is your every post online, and your commentary in real life, a moan, a dig, a world of negativity? Then don't expect others to come back for more. My blog honestmum.com is composed of my words, and of other writers' words I personally admire and feel will resonate with my audience. I operate an open-door policy where writers can pitch to me to feature. This offers them my platform and PR, while supplementing my site with super content.

Collaborate, don't compete, with those you admire. Competition should be healthy. The only person I compete with is myself, but admittedly I've been hurt by the jealousy of others, the sting of naysayers, and I've been shown time and time again who my real friends are. That's OK though. It's positive to know where you stand with others. It never stops me from trusting new friends or joining forces with others. It simply strengthens my armour and reminds me not to doubt my gut.

Setting up an online business/blogging can feel like solitary work, particularly at the start. We all need friends and colleagues to brainstorm with and also for reciprocal support. So, I urge you to consider your attitude to others, to question how you approach those working in your own field. To spin the negative and create positivity where possible, to conjure ways to come together, to be better, stronger and more successful as a team. To cut out those who try to kill your vibe and bring you down. To never focus on those who drain you and let their negativity in. Global brands and stars collaborate, why shouldn't you? They know that speed is king and that more brains equal greater content and the potential to break new ground and discover answers to problems quicker. It's no surprise that ensemble stars, groups or even YouTubers fair better together than on their own. Reach is amplified and so is the final product and impact.

Connect with others. Ask yourself how you can help one another, share ideas, contacts and expertise. Can you interview those you admire on your blog? Can you run a competition to support your mate's start-up? Can you RT (retweet) and share content from others regularly? Don't ask what others can do for you. Start by being proactive and help people you respect first. In short, stop being scared and start making the first move. What's the worst that can happen? Someone says no? Keep going until you hear yes. Someone will eventually say it!

STOP COMPARING

Why compare yourself with others?
No one in the entire world can do a better job of being you
> *than you*

UNKNOWN

One of the biggest zappers of confidence, and one of the key contributors to the imposter syndrome (where you believe yourself to be a fraud, whatever your achievements), is comparison. The act of comparing yourself to others can be soul-destroying. Yet we all do it, don't we? We compare ourselves to our peers, fellow creatives, mates, family members, neighbours ... and no more so than right now, with the all-pervasive, highly curated, mega-edited slice of life known as social media.

The art of comparing ourselves to others has gotten so much easier than peering over your neighbour's wall in the olden days (!), with Facebook and Instagram making it commonplace to snoop and inevitably feel crap about yourself with a single swipe. Being online has connected us in so many life-changing ways, yet, ironically, it's also driven huge divides between us, making us feel more self-critical, vulnerable and less successful than we are in reality.

The truth is that, while online life has made everything a little bit more hyperreal, comparison would happen regardless. We mustn't forget that competition is necessary and vital. It is the main mechanism for evolution. Evaluating and measuring ourselves against others will never phase out, nor should it, but equally it mustn't destroy or deter us either. That's never been its purpose. Competition exists to motivate and encourage greatness; it promotes the survival of the fittest, a world that thrives. Be inspired by others and unravel what they are doing so you can improve yourself. Can you up your photography game, spend longer writing posts, research areas in greater depth or discover new angles to share?

Weighing ourselves up against each other has been ingrained since childhood thanks to formal education, yet we so often forget that 'healthy competition' was what was always being advocated (or should have been): the window in which you can win and lose in an emotionally and physically safe environment, learning and growing while discovering what it takes to succeed.

That need to learn and improve must never be extinguished – it's the lifeblood of creativity and business too – but being kinder to ourselves and happy for others is critical to mental health, and success at work and at home. There is also a distinction between healthy and unhealthy competition. The former, which can reveal itself through the natural emotions of envy or emulation, encourages growth and creativity; the latter, worthlessness and jealousy.

You are fully in control of how you let others make you feel (that's adulthood for you): you get to decide your emotional response. The more you practise a healthy, positive response to pretty much anything (even adversity), the more you'll go on to action and to achieve positive results (rather than stuffing yourself with chocolate and hating the world forever). It's not too late to feel that way yourself, whatever your upbringing and role models. Believe me, I understand how hard it is playing our lives out online. A comparison-free life is not possible. It's not the way of the world.

I do believe it's a human instinct to favour sharing the good times over the bad. It's survival mode (at its prettiest) and I personally love reading about others' achievements. I want to see more women championing themselves. If all you do is play out the negative voices in your head, you'll drown out anything positive, manifesting a self-perpetuating cycle of low confidence in which you've literally lost the ability to track your progress. Know that when those, 'I'm just not good enough and everyone is better than me' feelings start boiling up, they're simply (loudly) telling you that you want a piece of greatness for yourself – be it autonomy, financial stability, travel, kids that smile in photos (!) or the perfect breakfast bowl. Regard that knock of confidence as a quiet siren building in order to wake yourself up so that you can focus on the aspects of your life that deserve your time and energy. Once you start to turn your mindset on its head you'll be so busy focusing on your own life, you'll stop thinking about others. You'll be so wrapped up in achieving your own goals, you won't have time to focus on what you don't have.

When it comes to social media and blogging – scrap that, when it comes to *life* in general – we only ever see the end result, never the graft, the blood, sweat and tears to get to that point/product/milestone. Don't compare your own page one to someone's one hundred and one. Those who do it well, who shine at all of the above (or seem to, most of the time), always make it look so easy. Making something look easy, though, takes time, consistency, hard work and determination. You have what it takes so go easy on yourself. Rome wasn't built in a day. OK!

PASSION + ACTION = SUCCESS

Just get back to the Passion + Action equation and you'll be on your way.

Five tips for getting over comparison paralysis

When you take action, even the first step towards a goal, it leads to feeling more confident. That confidence will build and build and spiral, soon becoming addictive and second nature. Here are my five top tips to help you when comparison paralysis hits, helping you to free-flow into greatness and productivity in your own way.

1. Get some context

Know that usually you're comparing the worst bits of your own life or recent experiences to others' perceived best bits. Try to garner a little context when you view people on social media at the coolest of parties, hanging with celeb mates or smashing career goals left, right and centre. We're all human, but it's easy to forget that we're the same. Life can be gloriously gorgeous and incredibly shit, and sometimes both at the same time.

Most people are good eggs, simply trying their best. They're not posting to piss you off: they simply want to share their lives and what they find meaningful because that's what people do. It's that, 'If we didn't photograph it, did it actually happen?' syndrome. We used to be all about sharing actual photos of holidays with our friends in person – now it's speaking to the whole world from our iPhones. And if you think that's full-on, then wait until virtual reality kicks in as mainstream and you're actually able to join those you follow on their dreamy holidays through your screen. (Will that help combat or exacerbate envy? Who knows?)

2. Strategise

Stop wasting time and energy on what others are doing and focus on your own game plan. Channel those forgotten hours scrolling timelines and living vicariously through your online heroes at 2am and start freaking *living* your own life or going to sleep or something! Start writing a plan of action. Observe what you like about others. Then strategise and create your own content. You love watching beauty YouTubers, but are not sure where to start? Watch the videos you enjoy, and the videos showing you how to recreate those videos. Film and edit on your phone at first, then move on to a vlogging camera, like the Canon G7X Mark II, and check out Adobe to cut your work.

3. Make a list of your awesomeness

When you catch yourself wishing you were someone else, remind yourself why you rock as you – just you. Even if you feel like a douche bag doing it, write a list in black and white (pen on paper – remember those?) of what you're most proud of and, in another column, a list of goals you want to make a reality.

Now start actioning those dreams, knowing that big results come from small steps.

Could you contact your local paper with a story on your last blog post? Can you get in touch with a brand you love via Twitter and pitch an idea to them? Could you crack on with that post you're scared to publish but you know will help others?

Can you simply be brave enough to start? Of course you can.

4. Remember: there's only one you

You are a one-off, an original and your unique voice will always distinguish you from others. The beauty of art is that being yourself and being genuine is what matters above all else. *Integrity is everything.* You must start to like and believe in yourself so that others will too.

Know that your viewpoint, your story, and the way that

you see the world is what others want to hear and read about. They want to see themselves reflected in your words, and that means being yourself – on the page as much as in person. We're all going through similar experiences as women/millennials/parents, and those universal themes will resonate and move others.

Organic search engine optimisation (SEO) means those interested in the same things you are, will find you, too. The internet is a beautiful thing.

5. Take some time out

If you're feeling totally overwhelmed and not good enough, take a break. Be kind to yourself. Go for a run, give yourself a digital detox for a while if you need to switch off. Bake a cake, paint – just do something else. Reflect on what matters by living in real life, offline.

We can easily become wrapped up in social media and literally forget the things right in front of us (hopefully a baked cake ready to be eaten!) and those who matter most. Also, don't feel a duty to follow those who don't make you happy. Unfollow and move on.

SEIZE OPPORTUNITIES

Always be proactive. I've never waited for success or expected it to come easily. Along with working hard, I've networked and emailed gatekeepers, journalists and PRs. I've grafted, safe in the belief that if you commit to growth and improvement, you can't be ignored forever – you will succeed. Take that approach too.

RETURNING TO EMPLOYMENT FEELING CONFIDENT

Getting back to work after maternity leave or a break can often feel unnerving. You've been away for what feels like an eternity and will need an acclimatisation period. The last time you were in work was most likely when you were pregnant and you now, no doubt, feel like a different person – particularly if you're a first-time mum. With Oliver, I know I felt like I was the first person in the world to have a baby!

The funny thing is, we're all creatures of habit and routine, and when that goes out of the window (when babies happen), we tend to crave normality and, often, our former jobs. I remember telling my GP at my six-week check-up that I was missing being a director. She agreed that she had felt the same when her twins were born and was desperate to get back to her patients. The downside to being freelance, however, meant that, unlike my doctor, I would need to go out and seek, pitch and hustle for work and I wasn't physically and emotionally ready to do that until much later. I definitely missed the ritual of my work life: planning my day, adult conversation, being creative and seeing projects come to fruition. It's OK and normal to miss your old life – and to be honest about that. Of course, not everyone feels that way. Many enjoy the freedom maternity leave brings, the new way of life. Some don't wish to return to work, ever, and that's OK too.

I think if I'd known I had something to return to, or a secure job that wasn't freelance and solely dependent on me as a creative, I would have worried far less during maternity leave. I would have embraced that time out of the work loop more. Maternity leave allows you to see how life could be outside of your current job or schedule. Many of my friends chose to return part time at first, moving back to full-time employment when their children got older. Others became stay-at-home mums and changed careers completely.

If you are returning to work, keep communication open and honest with your employer. Enquire about flexible working hours and job shares. Have a frank discussion about your needs. If your employer offers this, attend Keeping in Touch days, so you don't feel disconnected from projects or work during your time off. Ease in gently if you are able to, starting back on half days if you can. Partners often shift and swap work roles when kids come along. Could yours?

When Sarah Tomczak, executive editor of *Red* magazine, had children, her husband took time out of his career to support hers.

'For me "having it all" means being able to combine the career I love with motherhood. Luckily, I have a husband who believes in equality – and who has taken time out of his career as a photographer, first to look after our girls, full time (we shared my maternity leave) when they were very young, and now to become a freelancer (he used to work full time at a museum).'

Her husband's flexibility meant Sarah could commit to working almost full time (she works a nine-day fortnight), happy in the knowledge her children are being cared for by someone who loves them as much as she does. The set-up also suits them both in other ways – Sarah likes the structure and camaraderie of office life, while her husband prefers variety and is happy to work alone. She says he's also far better at housework than her.

The guilt still bubbles away though:

'This doesn't completely wipe out my maternal guilt. On the rare days I don't make it home by bedtime, I feel bad for all of us. And actually, a lot of my guilt shifts to my husband, simply because I know how relentless parenting can be and that a day at work is often the easier option.'

Sarah adores her job as a journalist and says that in many ways it brings her as much satisfaction and joy as motherhood:

> 'I have worked very hard to get where I am and I also recognise how lucky I am to get paid to do something I love. It's also important for me that my girls see my success – that they understand the value of hard work, the thrill of doing something you enjoy and that women can be the breadwinners just as much as men can.'

Getting back on set when Oliver was one was an emotional time for me. I felt guilty I was working away from him and, while directing didn't work for my little family in the long term, it gave me a taste of the creative life I had missed and still loved after a long maternity leave.

The juggle will inevitably feel tough when you get back to work life, but Tara Mohr, author of *Playing Big* (taramohr.com) has some invaluable advice:

> 'At work, try to get as much of your work as possible to be the things that really tap your unique strengths and gifts, with other team members doing what they – not you – are best suited for. At home, get help – especially with household tasks. And, think about what kinds of activities with your kids aren't just "shoulds" for you, but tap into your passions and loves too – is it doing art or music with them, or volunteering, or bringing them into nature – or what? Bring your real self and your particular interests to your time with them. That will make it both more special for them and more energizing for you.'

It might well feel like you're starting school again when you return to work, but you'll soon slot back in again. Try not to feel inadequate about your maternity cover. Rationalise why it was necessary. You couldn't physically be at work, so someone had to take your place. This wasn't personal. Remind yourself of your attributes and why you are good at your job. Be kind to yourself. It will take a little time for work life to feel familiar again, but most of my friends said that by the end of their first week, they felt like they'd never left.

Five top tips for returning to employment

1. Ease in gently

Do half days initially if you can, or make your first day close to the weekend so you'll have a break after the first day or two back. Don't be scared to ask questions or to set calendar reminders until you get back into the swing of things. Your colleagues will appreciate your needing support as you return to work.

2. Prep meals in advance

Freeze food for the week and do an online shop, which can help with meal planning. Make soup and one-tray bakes, which are great to freeze, as well as being healthy and filling. A roast at the start of the week can create lots of meals throughout, from salads to soups. Arrange packed lunches from the night before for yourself, and even plan your outfit, as well as your baby's, so the mornings feel less stressful.

3. Get some structure back into your life

For two weeks before returning to work, set your alarm so you get used to waking up at a specific time. Try to keep to that, even on your weekends – or days off, if you are going back part time – to help with structure. Sync your diary with work's and your partner's, noting any special days and events. Buy a huge wall calendar and hang it up, so you don't forget key dates.

Routine is important for you, as much as your child, so try to stick to going to bed at the same time every night to help prepare for being back at work. Whatever you do, know that things will feel a little surreal at first. That's normal. Soon enough, though, you'll get back into the flow of being at work and on projects that stimulate you. You'll feel excited and challenged, and you might well feel like I do – that being at work is the easy bit. It's the days off or the weekends, when little people are screaming, that are the hardest!

4. Don't let mum guilt win

The biggest challenge for most parents returning to work, or starting their own business, is the incessant wrestling with manic mum guilt. This often arises from now dividing your time between work and kids, and not being as readily available as you were on maternity leave.

Psychologist Dr Karen Pine, co-founder of Do Something Different Ltd (dsd.me), lends her advice on dealing with this:

'I honestly believe there's too much emphasis on the effects – positive and negative – of parental behaviour on children. Mothers worry that anything they say or do will impact upon their child, hence they're always worrying about getting it wrong and doing some lasting "damage".

I would say to mothers, let yourself off the hook a bit, stop beating yourself up. Of course, if you neglect or abuse your child it could do lasting damage, but mostly, if you love and care for them, they will be OK! Every minor decision does not have to be fraught with worry or potentially guilt-inducing.

There's some strong research showing that how children turn out as adults is influenced by their peer group more than their parents.

And recent research has also shown that to a certain extent, children's personality characteristics are 'contagious' i.e. they get them from their friends. It's time we told parents they can chill a little and mums can stop feeling guilty. If your child's a horror, it may be nothing to do with you!'

5. Say no

One thing I'm personally not great at is saying 'no' – the people-pleaser in me dies a little every time I do, but I've learnt the hard way (hi there, exhaustion) that no's are necessary if you want to keep your sanity. So that's my advice. Simplify your life and don't overstretch yourself. Life is about to change.

Five top tips on planning a new business

For those not returning to work, but opting for the entrepreneurial hot seat, here I share my tips for success.

1. Plan!

Do your research, plan and plot, and reach out to everyone and anyone who could help with insight. The British Library's Business and IP Centre at St Pancras, London, offers a huge range of free or low-cost events and workshops, as well as regular webinars, which can help you grow your business, so check out their website for more info (bl.uk/business-and-ip-centre).

2. Save

Make savings so you feel less pressure when launching, and know you have x amount to live on, for however long. Provide yourself with a financial cushion so the risk feels calculated. Also make provisions and back-up plans in case things don't go as you anticipate. Can you create a contingency plan? I always had a teaching career that I loved and could fall back on if freelance directing gigs dried up. Many women don't have a choice either way. I feel lucky that working has been an option for me, that my childcare costs and the support I had from my family meant that I could grow my business early on, transferring from a part-time blogging career to a full-time one over a few years.

Not everyone is in the same boat, so don't compare yourself to others, and simply do what you can in the time that you have. You will still succeed, it just might take longer. Put some money aside for a camera and website design, as investing from the start means approaching your business as the professional enterprise it will become. Looking slick is half the battle.

3. Create a flexible schedule and work in 'downtime'

Schedule time to work on your 'dream career' that fits around the job you currently have. This might mean waking up earlier in the morning or burning the midnight oil, but keep the bigger picture in mind as your motivator. Mine is a move to LA, running a global business, and directing a movie or two, please. It doesn't matter if I don't achieve those goals, it's the *big dream* that keeps me slogging. We all need a dream.

4. Practise self-care

Don't run yourself into the ground. There's no point to anything if you do. Don't forget to smell the roses, book a blow dry (or whatever makes you happy) and catch up with your mates. This new way of life is meant to be fun too, you know.

5. Reach out

Lean on friends and family for emotional support, and share the load with others. Accept help when it's offered and don't feel guilty about it. You are not Superwoman, OK? Superwoman is fictional, remember!

If you can afford a weekly cleaner, hire one. If you can put your kids in after-school club by making savings elsewhere, helping you to grow your business and eventually give you more freedom down the line, then do it.

Confidence boosters

Whether you are returning to work or starting your own business, these confidence-boosting tips have got you covered.

Visualise/ask the universe

Visualise your goals and ask the universe for the things you'd like to happen. This helps you to focus, gives you purpose, hones your passion and puts your declarations out there, motivating you to take action. You might feel crazy, but it works. The universe listens and once you put the work in, things will fall into place.

Silence your inner critic

Speak to yourself as you would your best friend. When self-doubt creeps in shout No or Stop. Be the friend you need and value in your life.

Silence outer critics

I'm not saying you should fill your circle with 'yes people'. We all need honest, genuine people who can be truthful with us, and we them, but it does mean ridding yourself of negativity – those who drain your energy and make you feel bad about yourself. Nobody's got time for that.

Try lots of things to find your passions

Be open to the joy of discovery. Let your love lead the way.

Work hard

Working hard achieves results. Once you find something you're passionate about, the working hard bit will feel easy.

Trust the timing of your life

Trust that things happen at the right time in your life. You are an active player in your life, but there's often a reason why you didn't pursue a particular path, or chose to change careers/cities/countries when you did. Trust that things will work out in the end and all will be well. Doors closing, blocks in the road and rejection encourage us to find new, innovative ways to succeed and teach us important lessons about our personality and what to do differently.

Be honest

My own self-esteem and feelings of self-worth are boosted when I communicate my feelings in a clear and candid way to others. That doesn't mean being rude or disregarding others' feelings – it just means being a genuine person. That way everyone knows where they stand with you, eliciting respect and trust.

Stop procrastinating, or waiting for the right time, because it won't ever come

Get a move on today. Take the first steps to changing your life by doing things that matter and that feed your soul. Importantly, know and believe with all your heart that you deserve success and happiness. Know your worth and demonstrate confidence from the off.

Here, author and leadership expert Eve Poole shares her confidence workout – tangible tips that have helped me before meetings, and even while writing this book:

'I bet you, like me, have days where you feel you aren't quite up to the task, and are bound to get found out at any minute. And the fear can be paralysing. So, what steps can you take to invest in your confidence, so you have more of it to draw on when you're feeling wobbly? Here is my five-point plan to make you a star!

1. True You
Let's start at the beginning. Knowing who you are gives you a "true north" you can turn back to when you feel disoriented. If you had to summarise yourself using just three words, what would they be? Don't worry if it takes you a while to pick the really true ones, but try a few on for size until you get your

perfect match. Let's say you pick "loyal, lucky and fun". When you next have butterflies waiting in a lift, or outside a door, or for a phone call, try the 'ten breaths' exercise. Listen to your breathing until it calms. Then 'breathe in' your words. For the first three breaths, say the first word to yourself; loyal, loyal, loyal. Then say the next one for the next three: lucky, lucky, lucky. Next: fun, fun, fun. For your tenth breath, breathe them all in: loyal, lucky, fun. Now, give yourself a smile. And go for it!

2. Your brand essence

In interaction, how you come across is actually more relevant than who you are. This sounds weird, but it's because the people around you won't necessarily ever get to know the true you, they just figure you out from the circumstances of the encounter. So, it's rather crucial to know how you tend to come across! Start by emailing seven people whose opinion you value and who know you well. Ask them to send you back three words that describe you. What can you learn from the similarities and differences between them? How do they compare with your "true north" words? Are there any words you didn't like? Can you ask for feedback on why they sprang to mind, and how you might attract a word you prefer? If you are feeling brave, ask them why they chose their words for you, and for examples of times when your behaviour has exemplified them.

3. Learning from your past

Find a piece of paper and try to chart your life like a timeline. Start by drawing a baseline across the middle of the paper from left to right. Then, starting from childhood, chart your life. Make the line go up when things were going well for you, and down when they weren't. Then have a look at all the high points you have captured. What made them such highlights?

What does that tell you about what is necessary for you to succeed? And what can you learn about your incredible resilience from all the bad times you have already managed to leave behind? What coping skills have you learned from your journey that you could use for your next wobble? And can you learn from your past about the early warning signs you need to heed in the future?

4. Designing out your fears

Now think about some of the goals you really want to achieve in life. What is currently standing between you and these goals? If any of them are about your fears, write down specifically what it is that you fear. Maybe it is a difficult conversation with someone? Or a skill you'd need to acquire? Or is it even how you look? Now try to break your fears down into baby steps. Is there something really small you could do in the next few days that would move you towards conquering these fears? Then what could you try? And what next? All of a sudden, you'll look round and find that you've arrived. Congratulations!

5. Legacy

Imagine that, in the future, someone is writing an appreciation of your life for a school alumni magazine. What would you like them to notice about you? What do you feel proud of already, and what else would you like them to be able to include in their article? Are there achievements you've yet to make that you'd like to press on with now? Or current priorities that need to shift? Or precious relationships that need more of your attention? You can write your own future; you just need to start that now. And remember, your body is made from stardust, so you are designed to shine!'

How empowering was that?

IMPOSTER SYNDROME

As a parent, it's easy to feel guilty that you're not doing enough, or that you're not doing it right. And, as a human being (and especially as a woman), it's easy to feel like you're an imposter – that you have no idea what you're doing, or how you've become successful. Both 'mum guilt' and imposter syndrome are my pet hates, and I've become something of an expert on how to deal with them (I was even on Sky News sharing my opinion on it): you overcome them both by handling your inner critic. That feeling of being a fraud is prevalent and no more so, I've found, amongst mums and those wanting to be mumbosses.

This self-sabotaging syndrome alludes to feeling like a fake when you have no reason to. It's something I suffer from (even when writing this book, as I questioned whether anyone would in fact read it, or if I had anything worth sharing). As you can see, I overcame that fear and you have, in your hands, the evidence that imposter syndrome can be beaten.

Other creatives empathise. Kate Thompson, author of a mighty seven books and *Sunday Times* bestselling novelist, suffers, too.

> 'I try to see negative, self-doubting chatter for what it is – a fabrication. I read recently that the voice in your head is not who you are, it's an excitable commentator. In other words, don't be held back by your perception of yourself. Mums can achieve great things, especially when they stop standing in their own way.'

The term 'imposter syndrome' was conceived by clinical psychologists Pauline Clance and Suzanne Imes in their 1978 study of 150 successful professional women in various fields when they discovered that, despite accolades, achievements and financial stability, many felt like frauds. Women are still subjected to sexism in this patriarchal society we live and work in, which is not helped by the inevitable shattering of confidence that can occur when kids come along, but our self-doubt can be beaten.

Psychologist Dr Karen Pine of Do Something Different (dsd.me) sheds light on why the imposter syndrome affects so many of us:

> 'I think it goes back to our feelings of self-worth. If we feel we truly deserve something we will nurture it. However, if we unconsciously feel that we're not worthy of something, or doubt that we're good enough, we may unwittingly sabotage it. The woman who cannot take full credit for her own success may rationalise it by saying, I got lucky, it was a fluke, or I had help. In other words, she attributes her success to factors outside herself, rather than making an internal attribution. This may lead her to fear that external factors will bring about failure in the future and by self-sabotaging she avoids having to face that.'

You *have to* acknowledge your achievements and experience. You must accept that you deserve success and that you have the same potential as everyone else. Tell yourself this right now. It's that simple, yet, of course, it's not that easy. It takes practice and time to feel worthy, particularly when you've lost your identity and are struggling with your place in the world, after children. I know, I've been there. Much in the same way that questioning your competence as a parent means you're actually a good one, self-doubt hits the most capable amongst us.

Women are susceptible to imposter syndrome because success makes us unlikeable – something backed by statistics. In the inspirational, must-read book *Lean In* by hero of mine, COO of Facebook Sheryl Sandberg, an experiment conducted in 2003 with business students is cited. The class of students was given the story of a successful entrepreneur; however, half the students were told the entrepreneur was called Heidi, while the other group was given the name Howard. Howard was considered likeable, talented and worthy of respect, yet Heidi was seen as selfish and not someone you would want to work for, or hire. Two identical profiles, the only difference being their gender. Granted those questioned were students, and not yet in the workplace, but it's rather telling, isn't it?

Things must change. Successful women should not be seen as somehow 'ruthless' or 'difficult', and we certainly don't need to act like the stereotypical hard-nosed male boss in order to thrive. I am testament to that. Pre-blogging days, I was a multi-award-winning filmmaker. I was always professional, honing the story and the performances of the pieces I led, yet I cared deeply too. I nurtured my cast and crew while remaining strong about my vision and leading a team. I was ambitious, as I am now, pitching for work, networking and putting myself out there, pursuing success, but not at the cost of anyone else. Being a bitch is not a default or characteristic of successful women, whatever the media might have told you.

In the early days, aged twenty-two, after gaining my MA, I worked for a famously tough movie boss and survived it. In fact, I more than survived it: I learnt, grew and grabbed and carved out opportunities, but it taught me a valuable lesson – that I wanted people who worked for, and with, me to feel happy and valued, not afraid.

I have never wanted to achieve at the expense of others. Instead, my filmmaking friends and I were dedicated to helping one another, recommending each other for work, sharing knowledge and contacts, and even regularly crewing up on one another's passion projects where possible. I do the same now as a blogger who collaborates and shares with others.

You must curb negative internal dialogue as it arises – it will prevent you from pushing higher and reaching your potential. Ambition is not a dirty word. Be assertive. Be you. Hold your head up high and remember that confidence is the destination, the ideal. It's *positive* to feel good in your skin, it's *Mecca*, so stop worrying that others might judge you if you appear happy and empowered, based on their own lack and yearning.

You have every right to *thrive*. So do they. Let your confidence create a movement that will filter down and ignite a spark in others. The more common it is to see strong women reflected back at us in the media (I'm looking at you, Beyoncé), the more we'll collectively feel it and, furthermore, will stop worrying that it might be confused with arrogance.

Women are directly and indirectly told from a young age not to be tenacious, to *not* 'lean in', speak up in class or take up their seat at the business table or in the director's chair, as Sandberg notes in her book. I wasn't that girl. With feminist parents who instilled self-belief in my brother and I from birth, I tend to feel pretty strong most of the time, no doubt because of that vital foundation. I have that constant reminder ringing in my ears, even now, that anything is possible. And that's despite teachers and employers who tried their best to silence me or change my personality. I fought to be me; to embrace the fact that I'm outgoing and talkative. Accepting and loving who I am made me successful.

Nonetheless, I'm human, creative and sensitive, and often experience times where my confidence wanes or dissipates entirely. I've had abuse, on- and offline, from others determined to pull me down or break my confidence. I've had lies and character assassinations published about me, but I don't let them stop me as I know who I am. I talk, cry and deal with the pain. It's the only way.

I'm now pretty good at the 'moving on' part: I forget easily, never hold grudges and press forward, not looking back. This attitude has materialised thanks to being in the media industry for many years, understanding rejection, dusting myself off after each and every mistake or adversity, and accepting that failure and criticism is a part of the process. Everyone must fail in order to ultimately succeed. We must all overcome negativity in order to feel strengthened.

I also have a new, greater appreciation of what success means to me: be it having more free time in my work week, achieving a contract with a brand I admire, or writing a blog post that resonates with others and makes a difference, however small that might be.

Success is fluid, and my kids, my greatest success of all, ground me when life feels crazy. I look at them and feel lucky and am reminded why I want to achieve: for those guys. That's the wonderful thing about being a mumboss. I remember being so overwhelmingly obsessed with directing my first feature film pre-children. Having Oliver, though, showed me what truly matters. He gave me balance in his own unbalanced way. In that respect, motherhood feels liberating. It allows me to chase my dreams because my biggest dream – becoming a mum – has already been met.

I do of course still suffer from the imposter syndrome occasionally. There are times I question myself, wondering if I'm the right person for the job, or whether someone, somewhere made a mistake in hiring me, but this is what helps me when it hits:

1. List your strengths and absorb them. We all have attributes to be proud of. Remind yourself of yours.
2. Learn that being proud of who you are and your achievements is not arrogance, it's healthy self-belief. There's a difference. You must learn to accept and believe in praise. When someone compliments you don't reject their words, say 'Thank you'.

3. Practise praise with your partner or a friend. Tell each other what you love about one another and breathe it in, believing every word to be factual. It's like learning to take compliments. It's easy to brush them off, but once you start thanking others when they praise you, it affects your self-esteem and has a positive knock-on effect on all that you do.

4. Don't be afraid to promote yourself and share milestones in your life and business. You no doubt like to hear of others' successes so why not share your own?

5. Do something kind for someone else for nothing in return – from offering a business contact to making an introduction or sharing their work. Nothing boosts wellbeing more than helping others.

I hope you feel empowered by this chapter and are willing to ride the rollercoaster of being a mumboss, because you'll probably feel brimming with confidence one day and sick to the stomach with self-doubt the next. It happens to us all. I know one thing for sure: I'm committed to trying my hardest to prevent imposter syndrome from making me feel like a fraud.

I'm not an imposter, and nor are you.

Chapter 4

HOW TO HUSTLE – BUILDING A BUSINESS FROM YOUR PASSIONS

We mothers are always hustling: working hard, working late, being there for assemblies and school trips, making hot dinners and simply trying our best. We're winging it mostly, but giving it our best shot. I'm a hustler, baby ... and so are you.

This chapter explains the importance of passion and how, once you find it, pivoting feels easy. The hustle is worth it. I also cover how to deal with trolls, naysayers and the importance of real friends for happiness and business success.

BEING A MOTHER-HUSTLER

It's such a dream scenario to see the digital industry boom. Seven years after I started, professional bloggers, vloggers, Instagrammers and internet business owners big and small are 'smashing it', with new sites and handles popping up each and every day (and no doubt every second). Luckily there's enough internet to go around for everyone. (Yay!) These individuals – now named 'influencers' – are also reaching huge financial heights, with many superseding their previous incomes and earning six or even seven-figure sums. How cool is that?

You will know the mumboss story well by now, but if you need reminding, here goes. We mother-hustling mamas have kids and then discover how limiting and inflexible our current workplace is, and that childcare is crazy expensive. We feel lost and desperately need to reclaim our identities and find a way to work that fits around our family because – *shock horror* – we actually want to spend time with the kids we made. We *want* to attend harvest festivals and take our kids swimming after school and be present for them, while combining parenthood with a stimulating and financially rewarding career. Is that too much to ask?

As much as motherhood can break us down at times, it can also build us up and give us the ammunition to survive: it enables the warrior instinct to prevail, whatever shit (literally) hits the fan. As all the mums I spoke to testified, while we might not feel strong at first, when that first flicker of confidence returns, it whets our appetite for more and before we know it, we're free-flowing and unstoppable, addicted to the thrill of simultaneously feeding our creativity and our babies. Setting up a site or shop online is an act of self-care, really. It's telling ourselves that we're valuable enough to own a piece of land online. That we deserve a space to write, create, film and share. That *we* matter. With each new post we write and publish, we grow a little and, soon enough, those posts accumulate and build a brand and a new identity. Maternity leave is a critical time for budding entrepreneurs, many of whom don't yet know they're entrepreneurs, budding or otherwise. I always advise that a new business, like a baby, needs nine months of nurturing to grow. Parental skills are transferable when it comes to business: juggling, problem-solving, mediating and hitting goals – be it keeping your baby fed, warm and safe or making that sale in business.

Whatever your circumstances, you can still create a flourishing blog. I know single parents who have done just that by night, as their kids sleep. Others, who work shifts, write during designated sleep time, or even when they commute to work. Some wake up before the rest of their house, as my friend Dr Juliet McGrattan did when writing her fitness book *Sorted*. Yes, the more frequently you blog and vlog, the quicker your business grows, but quality is key and blogging twice a week consistently will be enough to see your blog gain pace.

And the best news? Your kids will be a constant source of inspiration for your blog or business, whether that's finding a gap in the market for your own line in gender-neutral clothing, setting up a site about the way you parent or feed your kids healthy meals, or a new-found love of fitness. Along with inspiration from your family, you'll find you can build a business relatively easily and quickly with a good dose of passion and tenacity.

WHAT TO BLOG ABOUT

Blogging inspiration can come from anywhere, but writing about what you know is a good place to start. Write what you would like to read yourself. It's always nerve-wracking to hit publish, especially when it comes to personal posts: it's an emotionally vulnerable thing to do, to share your thoughts and experiences with the world. That honesty, however, is powerful and will be cathartic for you and those who read it. I turned my trauma, rage and pain into ideas and videos. I simply shared my heartbreak. I processed and, in turn, helped others by finding the courage to share. We need honest voices; people who are unafraid to be human and vulnerable, publicly. There are many ways to be a mother too, and blogs reflect this. Blogs help destroy stereotypes and limitations.

Make life simple

When you write about your passions, you'll never be short of inspiration. I love food, Mediterranean food in particular, as well as making healthy versions of cakes I adore, so those are two areas I focus on. Fashion and travel also feature heavily in my blog, along with family life. Editorial leads to advertorial opportunities, so the more you write about a subject, the greater the chance you'll also be commissioned by brands in those 'lanes'. Not limiting myself to one genre or topic, and operating as a lifestyle blog that combines my many interests, has naturally led to work in lots of sectors. The more I cover, the greater the commissions.

Don't feel you need a niche. You are your niche! Your voice, your style, the way you shoot your photography and literally live your life are all a personal reflection of you and your brand. Remain true to your values and ensure that you do not lose the trust of your audience. Readers must always know where they stand with you.

Approach your blog as you would a magazine

When I started, I thought about what I enjoyed most in newspapers and magazines and based my blog on those preferences, incorporating interview features, style spotlights and opinion pieces. I wanted it to be eclectic and engaging.

Once you write a blog post, review the piece, reading it out loud to check flow and tone. Ensure grammar and punctuation are spot-on, too. Don't limit yourself tonally either. If you only write comedic-style posts, for example, you might feel a pressure to always entertain, even when you don't feel like it.

Simply be yourself, writing frankly and concisely.

Posts that are too long can be off-putting (remember your reader is busy) and those that are too short might fail to engage. Use memorable visuals and create content that consistently reflects your personality and signature style, so it's recognisable anywhere.

Vitally, share your experiences and expertise. Don't keep what you know, and that might help others, close to your chest. I was one of the first parenting bloggers to share exactly how I made a living blogging and vlogging, giving advice on how others could follow suit. By doing so, I became an expert and leader in my field. Whether you have unique style tips or recipes, parenting advice or experience in finance *share, share, share.* People will then pay for that experience, directly or indirectly, they will buy your products, clothes, books etc. Importantly, by giving away your know-how for free on your blog, you will be repaid by views, which will lead to paid work from brands. It's a win–win situation.

Struggling with what to write about? Tara Mohr, acclaimed leadership expert and author of *Playing Big* will inspire you:

'I would say that great writing comes out of the combination of two opposite things: 1) writing consistently – daily or close to daily and 2) stepping away from the desk and living your life. This is such an interesting combination. We need the consistent writing to practise, to get nimble with words, and to write enough that we become less attached to any one thing we produce – able to discard, cut, and edit freely.

Yet what we do at the desk is only part of the equation. The gold of emotion, insight and truth-telling that makes writing great comes from what happens in our lives – the difficult conversation we choose to have, that emotional risk we take with a loved one, the piece of art we took in from another artist, the time we took to pursue our own thinking about a topic.

We have to live conscious lives to have material to write about, and we have to write regularly to be able to articulate that material well.'

You might even find yourself running two blogs, each one supporting the other. My mate Mirka Moore did just that, launching an inspirational health and fitness site, Fitness 4 Mamas (fitness4mamas.com), several years after establishing a successful parenting blog, All Baby Advice (allbabyadvice-blog.com). Her fitness blog grew rapidly thanks to her existing personal brand and the ability to cross-promote between both sites, widening her reach and appeal.

Your own blog (or blogs) is there for the taking. It's not some whimsical dream or pie-in-the-sky notion. With consistent sharing, you can build a personal brand with purpose. You already have the skills you need thanks to raising a baby.

Parenthood changes you. How could it not? I remember my baby choking as they tend to do when first eating solids. Your life stops in that frantic moment as you try to get the food out or down. You live for that child of yours. I've literally thrown myself in front of a car for my kid (Oliver ran in front of a car at a supermarket when he was three). I would die for my kids. Those powers to nourish, love and protect, however scary the circumstances, are transferable business skills. You can learn to compromise and will adapt too. I am often arranging school uniform and sports kits at 2am if I've had a late deadline. You know hard work because that's life with kids.

Not only do children offer you context so that you don't get too wrapped up in the minutiae and pettiness day-to-day work life can bring, but they also teach you the act of juggling so that you can learn to prioritise and exist on little sleep. I defined myself by my career pre-kids, but children changed my path. No one can predict where your blog might take you.

THE STANDARD WORK DAY
DOESN'T SUIT PARENTS

It was heart-breaking to be apart from my son for even half an hour after maternity leave, let alone weeks at a time as a director, which was what was required of me. I wanted to work and return to my former creative life, but my personal circumstances had changed and I needed to accept that working away from my son just wasn't an option for me. It was affecting my wellbeing. Thank goodness that my passion project, my blog, became a means to provide for my family.

First-time motherhood, while stifling and drowning me in a mess of sleep deprivation and haywire hormones, eventually reignited my creativity. It got me back on track. It gave me purpose again when I thought I had none. Perhaps it was down to the fact that my creativity was desperate to release itself, after initially being dampened when my eldest was born – or maybe it arose because I'd created my greatest, most challenging piece of art whom I loved unconditionally: Oliver!

It's funny, really. How can someone so small and disempowering in so many respects eventually give you so much strength? That's the irony of motherhood. It's like the way muscles tear during exercise, only to become stronger for it: they have to break to be rebuilt. Many women find that they start to re-evaluate their careers during maternity leave. Lucy Griffiths, author of *Dream It, Do It, Love It* (lucygriffiths.com), was one of those:

'A friend told me to use my maternity wisely . . . I thought she was clearly bonkers. I was utterly exhausted, and, having a little one suctioned to my breast, I thought she was talking nonsense. But in time, I began to realise that she was right, it just took me a while to figure it out. Here's some things you can do even when you feel exhausted: listen to audio books to learn things to develop your mind, or help you grow a business while you walk in the park, read books on your iPhone or kindle while you snuggle with your little one, and use your time to imagine how life could be if you didn't have to do the daily commute, and could quit the 9–5. Use this time to start dreaming, start planning and start creating!'

Having babies can bring upheaval, but as I've experienced myself, becoming a mum can boost creativity and offer clarity and purpose. I love that my digital career allows me to be present for my kids while doing a job I adore. Multi-award-winning filmmaker and actor of film and TV Manjinder Virk shares how kids affected her:

'It is difficult to put down in words how much having children changes your life and ultimately your understanding of the world and your place in it. For me, finding a way to balance work with my home life was crucial and remains so. Both my husband and I are freelance so we take it in turns to make sure one of us is always there for the children. They remain at the centre of how we live and work. Even when it seems impossible, we find a way.'

I've found the less time you have, because of kids, the easier it is to prioritise. I want to achieve, succeed and be happy – for my children, as much as myself, now. They are my driving force. And to do that, I have to hustle: I have to not feel scared to put myself out there and share my own life, fears and honest take on the world, and to pursue what I want from my career and life. I don't have time to lose. There are mouths to feed. I have to make my career and life *happen*, not while away time being unproductive.

You see we're all hustlers, whether we're trying to get our kids to sleep, send that email, create a business plan or, most importantly, make others believe in us and have them see what we're capable of bringing to the table. And that's never more key than when we've lost our confidence after having kids and must coax it back, so we can become contenders in the ring again.

There are now more entrepreneurial mums than ever. Many will have developed their ideas while on maternity leave, seeing a gap in the market or a window of opportunity to finally get their dream businesses or careers off the ground, and just went for it. Rites of passage, and even adversity, can fuel ambition. When you are down and suffering, it can be hard to imagine normality will ever resume. When it starts to, so does a renewed zest for life and grabbing it by the horns, appreciating every minute. This was the case with Laura Bonnell of kidswear brand The Letterman Co. (lettermanco.com). Her story is both moving and inspiring:

'During my second pregnancy I was diagnosed with a malignant melanoma when I was 5 months pregnant. I managed to have a small operation on it while I was pregnant, but had to wait until I had the baby to return for further surgery to see if the cancer had spread. Two weeks after he was born I went back for surgery, and then had to wait a further 2 weeks for the results. Fortunately, the cancer hadn't spread, and I was then put on 3 monthly check ups. Not too long after that my father suddenly got ill while on a trip to France. He was admitted to hospital and a couple of days later we discovered he had pancreatic cancer, and it had spread to his liver. Unfortunately, it was too late to do anything. Sadly 2 weeks later he passed away...'

A few weeks later Laura was called into a meeting with her director at work and told she was losing her job – and just before Christmas, the first without her dad. She recalled that, after a short pity party at the local pub with her husband, she decided she wasn't ever going to let someone hurt her like that again.

'I've wanted to be a fashion designer all my life, but I was going to do it on my terms! The next week I got sketching and sewing, and I took myself along to a local networking meeting. I turned up with a cushion I made, my ideas and my details printed out on pieces of paper – because I hadn't had a chance to make business cards! After getting some positive feedback, I decided to go for it, and I made some more things, set up my website, and then started telling more people about my company. I was ideally placed in south-west London (also known as Nappy Valley because of the high concentration of kids) to research and target my market. Word quickly spread, and I managed to build up the business, and quickly outgrew the office pod we had at the end of our London garden!'

Last year Laura decided to finally put into action her dream of moving to California. If the events of the previous year had taught her anything, it's that life is too short, and she and her family decided to follow their dreams. They sold their flat, put all their worldly possessions into a 20-ft shipping container, and moved to Orange County in Southern California!

'I've had to almost start again with Letterman Co. over here, and I can't say it's been easy! Setting up a small business is not a straightforward exercise, but I am getting there. The e-store is back open, I've got some markets under my belt, and I'm about to do my first Pop Up Shop. I've even been approached about a reality TV show, and I'm filming the pilot next week! Life is full of opportunities, you just have to go out and find them. This is the hardest I've ever worked (and I'm a work horse), but I love every minute of it, and I know this is what I am supposed to do.'

Kids can be the impetus for switching things and inspiring you to achieve your dreams. Zaz Grumbar changed careers after parenthood, from being a senior marketing manager in the perfume industry to setting up a blog, and then again to become a yoga teacher (yogawithzaz.com), pivoting twice. After a fifteen-year career in fashion and beauty, she felt a shift after having children and readdressed her new needs.

'One day I looked up and realised the demands of my job meant I was seeing my kids for less than 2 hours every working week and the nanny was earning more than the mortgage. I took a deep breath and leapt off the corporate ladder, followed my heart and trained as a yoga teacher. It wasn't easy to re-evaluate my sense of self without a big salary and fancy title, but I realised swiftly how much happier I was and am to work in a way that means I call the shots, work hard and genuinely affect people. It has taken a little while, but financial independence and a deeply settled sense of self is a reality that has come with hard work, and it is possible without being confined to the constructs of a traditional career path.'

HOW TO RECOGNISE WHEN YOU ARE READY TO PIVOT

You won't know what you're passionate about unless you consistently try new things. You won't know that you're capable of getting back to work until day one, when you start again. It's time to embrace a new normal.

First, ask yourself whether you need a change right now. Do you want to plunge into a new industry or give life to a new business idea? Do you want to change careers, pivoting from your current job, or do you want to branch out from your career, adding another business to the mix?

Sarah Willingham, a serial entrepreneur, mum of four and former dragon on BBC Two's *Dragons' Den* advocates asking yourself why you are doing this business, why it's important to you and why it matters. Then you should ask yourself why it makes you happy. She feels so many people get caught up in running a business, that they forget to examine their motivations.

Sarah feels that asking yourself why helps you to remain focused on your goals when things get tough. She reminds us that it should be enough to tell yourself that you deserve to follow your career goals and that this doesn't make you a 'bad mother'. It's about feeding your own creative needs, nourishing yourself, and by doing so, your family too:

> 'You can't do it all, so don't even try! Work out what's important to you and focus on that, whether that's going back to work or choosing to be a full-time mum. Once you've worked it out, give that 100% of your energy and focus rather than trying to do lots of things only half right. Mama ALWAYS knows best – trust your instinct.'

Natasha Courtenay-Smith, digital strategist and author of *The Million Dollar Blog* (natashacourtenaysmith.com), feels that the digital world is liberating and is glad she embraced tech as a career:

> 'I always knew working digitally would be freeing. Back in my more 'corporate' life working at a newspaper, I used to think I would never be able to have children and continue that way of working because things like the hours, the commute, the unexpected calls from my boss, having to work weekends just didn't fit with motherhood.'

Natasha left her job before really reaching a point where she was feeling broody at all, and set up her first online business. She said she knew she did want children one day, and the goal was to be able to reach a point where she had established and scaled the business before kids, rather than having to do that after children.

She fell pregnant the very first week the website went live, so only had nine months to establish and scale the business. By the time her first child was born she had a small team of two running the business for her. Although there were many highs, and a few lows, she said it was ultimately run to her rules. Its office was based a five-minute walk from her house (and when she moved house she moved office), and both were a five-minute walk from the nursery. She used to joke that she never left this small triangle of London in which her three key points were five minutes apart, but it was the only way she could continue running and building a business while still having what she considered a good amount of time with her children: 'For me, I still wanted to work and have a good career, but to finish work just before five and to be able to do the drop-off and pick up at both ends of the day.'

Natasha sold her business in 2014 and has since written her book and set up a creative digital agency. The agency, called Bolt, helps people and businesses become better known for what they do – from the launch, scoping, branding, and photography and website builds through to website management and content across a variety of media forms and platforms, as well as publicity. Her clients range from celebrities to entrepreneurs and those running stately homes, and she speaks at events as well as mentoring individuals one to one.

'Again, the most important thing is that working digitally allows me flexibility. It's also creative, fun and I know we do a great job for our clients. People think I am crazily ambitious and I am ambitious to some degree. But also, what I'm interested in is having a nice life, not being stressed, working to my own hours and doing a good job for my clients.'

She feels there is no way she could have the time with her kids like she does now if she was in a traditional job.

'What is funny is that my kids still moan at me that I'm 'always working'! This isn't true! I always say to them, 'I'm here every morning, every early evening, I don't commute, I rarely travel.'

Natasha also tells her children that her whole life has been deliberately set up for them and that she got organised for them, even before either of them were conceived. When they are older and look back, Natasha knows they will realise she did an all right job of balancing things as best as she could, given that she wanted to build her career – and that the internet and working digitally have been pivotal to facilitating that for all of them.

Women are noticing opportunities and feeling they could meet the needs of other mums like them, then turning those ideas into businesses. Food blogger Vicki Montague at Free From Fairy (freefromfairy.com) launched her own flour when she saw a gap in the market.

'I set the Free From Fairy up as a blog in 2012 to teach people how to eat healthily while on a restricted diet due to allergies or intolerances to food. My daughter was diagnosed with allergies to milk protein and eggs in 2008 and then with coeliac disease in 2010 at the age of 2. I wanted to share my free from recipes with others in our situation and to make life easier for my daughter when she visited friends and family who didn't know how to cook for her.'

Using her science degree, Vicki spent years developing a multi-purpose, wholegrain gluten- and rice-free flour blend. When baking with existing blends, Vicki found that her daughter was always hungry, as these were made from refined white flours. Her blend provides vital fibre, protein and micronutrients, without relying on rice, which is so prevalent in gluten-free food. In 2016, with encouragement from her blog readers, she brought the flour blend to market, initially, she said, as an experiment to fill a gap in the market.

'I was utterly terrified when I launched it at the Allergy and Free From show in London; years of hard work had gone into it and I felt so exposed. Having turned 40 the same year I decided that it was time to just do things without over thinking them (a problem that I've always had). My advice to anyone thinking about doing something is to consider the following two things:

1. Can you afford to do it? What would the consequence be of it not working in terms of money?

2. Can you afford not to do it? How would you feel on your deathbed if you didn't do it?'

Vicki said she didn't look too far ahead when she answered the first question. She knew she could afford to create one batch and test it on the market and decided she would make it work beyond that – not overthinking things, and instead just doing them. She said that, while this is probably not the advice that a business advisor would give, it worked for her!

'They might tell you to write a business plan, look at projections and all sorts of other things but that didn't work for me.

At this stage in my life I felt that action and "learning on the job" was the way forward. It brings its challenges but if I'd tried to plan it all out I never would have done it ... it would have seemed way too scary and big.'

Her biggest piece of advice to other mums looking to become a mumboss is to look at the immediate risks and, if they seem manageable, to take that step forwards boldly, as nobody ever gets anywhere without being brave! She says she has days when she feels extremely unconfident, but surrounding herself with positive, inspiring people helps build that back up again.

Importantly, she advises not being afraid to try something out and changing tack if it doesn't work out. Feeding your soul must take priority. If you don't like something, change it.

My friend Nomita Vaish-Taylor, founder of an award-winning interiors blog (yourdiyfamily.com), advises that we mustn't be scared to change direction or quit something that doesn't feel right. It's the only way to prosper. You try something out and if it makes you unhappy or doesn't succeed, you take on board the lessons and apply it to something else. No experience is wasted:

'I'm a big believer in trying new things. I felt a real pull towards Korean children's fashion and so I started an e-shop. Even though the shop was doing well, a year or so into it I realized that retail wasn't for me. It took me a little while to accept this but once I did, I knew the right decision was to close the shop and I did just that, focusing on my DIY blog.'

Try things out and if they don't work, move on and try something else.

FINDING YOUR TRIBE AND DEALING WITH NAYSAYERS AND TROLLS

I couldn't do what I do without the love and support of family, friends and colleagues. Those guys who endlessly buoy me up, help me develop my work, give me honest feedback and back me emotionally whenever I doubt myself. They respect and support my vision, and always keep me going. My husband Peter is my rock and sounding-board and he shares the load right down the middle when it comes to childcare, shoulders to cry on, school pick-ups, meals and more. He's also the first person I go to when things go wrong.

The thing is, putting yourself out there online takes guts, and sometimes people grab at those guts of yours, twisting them into knots, bruising you so badly you feel like giving up. We've all been there. Mean girls (and guys), otherwise known as trolls or naysayers, are the dark side to sharing your life online and, while you do build a resistance to this over time, as sensitive creatives it's normal to feel hurt by cruel words and untruths.

In the seven years that I've been blogging, I can't say I've had it relentlessly tough, but I have certainly experienced my fair share of nastiness. There was an incident on Twitter when a troll slated my children, I was body-shamed after my second baby, and even had vile libel published about me not long ago. Every insult has been an opportunity to grow in strength, though – to rise again, stronger than before. Admittedly, our all-too-frequent preoccupation with what others think of us is part of human nature, but it often feels exacerbated a million times over in the online world. There, everyone is free to share their opinion (fine) or worse, troll others (not fine), as and when they wish, based on assumptions and often lies. A win for a democratic, decentralised internet, yes, but a complete and utter fail for virtual and real-life bullying.

I often hear blogger friends complain that others have tried to manipulate their words or destroy their confidence online, and I've experienced it myself. The jealousy of others can be so strong that they seem committed to the cause of destroying you, but integrity and honesty always prevail so don't forget that. We must lead by example and act in a way that our own children would be proud of. It is our duty to be purveyors of justice. More so, we must not allow others to prevent us from doing what we love because they envy our passion and determination. We cannot let the opinions of strangers cloud our own judgement, ruin our morale or paralyse our passion.

The years have fortified me and, for the most part, I take no heed of those who don't know me. I feel free. In the way that a bully relies on you to yearn for his/her approval, once you stop seeking that consent from strangers, you immediately garner respect, purely because you know and respect yourself.

I think hearing my dad refer to me as a success had a profound effect on me. The little girl in me high-fived the thirty-seven-year-old I am now. And that's it too: I suppose reaching my thirties has been a landmark in terms of understanding who I am and what I want – and being careful about the energy that surrounds me. I have a strong network of real friends and, as always, a hugely supportive family. The only time I *am* ruthless is when it comes to negativity and cutting it out. If people or situations consistently prove destructive, I've gotten good at walking away. I'm also pretty good at self-reflection and holding my hands up when I mess up. We're all infinitely flawed but life is about making sense of that and trying to be the best you.

Sharing our lives and those of our families can mean facing unfair criticism and trolling, so it's critical to grow a thick skin and ultimately stop letting what others think of you eat you up. You must relearn the negative behaviour of being obsessed with others' views. Let out the sadness but then draw a line under it. Discussing trolling with fellow creatives helps me feel less alone. The key is not to ignore your feelings, but to ignore the naysaying perpetrators. It's time to work on your self-worth and bear in mind a saying my friend Harriet Thorpe often reminds me of, 'what other people think of you is none of your business'. We must not allow others' opinions of us to mould or cloud our own. It is important that I add, though, how much I *do* value the opinions of those I trust.

Those I feel close to are 100 per cent honest with me and tell me when I'm wrong and I, them – and that's the key to strong relationships: accepting the warts and all, having each other's backs, but, for me, also telling it like it is and being an 'honest mum'. No one is perfect. We're all just trying our best with the end goal of being content. Not worrying what others think of you does just that – it sets you free and makes you happy. Someone doesn't like or understand you? That's OK. Someone assumes things about you, or jumps to conclusions? Who cares? You shouldn't. We all view people and situations through the eye of our own experiences and, more often than not, our own baggage. Try not to judge others and don't sweat those who judge you.

You know you, and that's what matters.

A controlled reaction

So, what happens when someone hits out at you? You control your reaction, that's what. Not easy, but with practice you'll soon feel like Buddha!

I'll be honest, I'm a stickler for justice. I find it hard to sit back and accept when people treat others, or indeed myself badly. I'm an advocate of standing up for yourself and your beliefs. I also have no interest or time for pettiness or one-upman/womanship and pride myself on getting on with most people. I'm kind, I empathise with others and appreciate differences, and I forgive (too much, my dad says), but I'm not a pushover either. It's a balance – empathising with others and making allowances for them while not taking shit either.

It's vital to remember that when it comes to how we process and react to others, the power is in our hands. Trauma, criticism and trolling are rampant, and we can react badly or angrily as they arise, or we can work on *choosing* our reaction: opting to be rational, calm, strong and even silent, if necessary, in the face of adversity. I'm not saying we should deny how we feel and not cry things out to those we trust, or be honest when someone has hurt us – bottled-up emotions are destructive – but we should choose our battles carefully and become savvy at working out what truly warrants getting upset about.

Yes, it's hard. Don't ask me to practise what I preach during PMT week, when I literally need to move to my own island (calls Richard Branson), but the rest of the time, I work at being calmer, however acute or trivial the scenario. When my kid draws on my freshly painted lounge walls? *Je suis calme*, 'Let's just use that extra paint for emergencies and cover that Minion-looking thing'. When the person who doesn't know me from Adam makes a disparaging comment on my blog, I take a deep breath, *accept* they literally don't know me from Adam, and move on. It's about accepting what you cannot change and trying to find a silver lining where possible – for example, that person writing about me still gave my blog a pageview! The encouraging, positive comments always outweigh the negativity. Keep a positivity file on your computer, where you store positive comments and emails, and open it whenever you're having a bad day. My supporters online always brighten my day and keep me blogging and vlogging.

I always like to remind myself of therapist, author and researcher Hillary McBride's (hillarymcbride.com) wise advice on dealing with naysayers and trolls when the going gets tough:

'When on the receiving end of hurtful or critical interactions, it can be helpful to remember the following: "hurt people hurt people". People who do not carry deep pain and fear about who they are, about others or about the way the world works, do not hurt other people intentionally. It's a function of their pain; their wounds as a person. So when someone hurts you, it is important to remember that their behaviour is about their own hurt and dysfunction in the world, not about your worth and value. And, remember that they are hurting something they think is an object, and you are not an object. You are three dimensional, and more than your online presence, and it is OK that it hurts when people do or say painful things. But, you also need to find a way to protect yourself against that. You might try saying that to yourself out loud as a way to remind yourself. Try to find ways to remind yourself about what is true about you, and integrate them into your life. Perhaps there is a poem that you can go back to or look at when you are hurt, or a piece of scripture or a proverb, or a letter from someone you love – something that grounds you in who you really are, not what they are saying about you. You might find it helpful to mount this near your computer, or set it as a home screen on one of your devices.'

I have personally found Lajos Egri's *The Art of Dramatic Writing* a useful insight into character and action. It made me less judgemental and more forgiving.

Friends forever

A vital word on friendship. Real friends are worth their weight in gold. I'm lucky that many of my closest friends are my oldest friends. They know me better than I know myself. Sometimes it's hard to know who to trust when you're public facing, but I always remain open to others while listening to my gut. Not everyone, as sad as it is to write, wants the best for you, and parents, who are sleep-deprived and more stressed out than most, might find that our radars can also be off kilter at times.

The key is to remember that real friendship shouldn't feel like hard work.

The first friendships I made in the blogging world are some of my strongest today. We celebrate one another's achievements and find collaborating a joy. I love seeing women, and men, shine, and feel proud to have helped many share their work more widely and get book deals and/or businesses off the ground. I don't just talk the talk, I walk the walk. As does my tribe.

Even if you don't work with your mates, you still need one another's support and advice in order to stay sane and prosper. True friends help you feel competent and able to combat the inevitable negativity on and offline.

Collaboration between fellow creatives means you can share skills, promote one another's work, share contacts and recommend each other for press and work opportunities. Reach out to those in the blogging community with whom you share values and interests. Equally, seek out those who can offer the skills you might lack yourself. Help each other and increase opportunities and pleasure tenfold.

Handling criticism

Alice Olins and Phanella Mayall Fine of Step Up Club (step-up-club.net) have insightful tips on handling criticism:

'Criticism, when dished out by Sir Alan's chums in the interview round of *The Apprentice* is criticism that has been made for TV. It's obnoxious and sensational – no one wants to be the target of that type of denigration. But criticism isn't as bad as it's cracked up to be ... Don't look at criticism like an unwanted guest at a work party; rather, think of it as a valid call to improvement.'

Having personally worked in the media industry since the age of sixteen (with my first work-experience slot being in local news), I learnt early on how to handle criticism, to not take it personally, to seek out what resonated and to commit to constantly improving. Try to detach yourself, and reflect on your work as objectively as possible, serving the company/project and not your ego.

Alice and Phanella advise asking these three questions when you receive criticism:

- Who gave it to me?
- What is your purpose?
- Why do I need you?

As my mum likes to remind me, 'You'll never please everyone,' and the sooner you realise this, the better. Not everyone will 'get' you, nor you them, and some might outright dislike you (and, when it comes to online life, often for no reason at all, or for trivial ones based on a single tweet or blog post), so it's important to gain some perspective. Stop sweating the small stuff and focus on what matters. You, your work and your family.

Here are my top tips on handling criticism like a boss. A mumboss.

The joy of it

I think when you remind yourself of the joy that you feel when you take action and create, the way it feels when you lose yourself in your words, you are better able to weigh up the pleasure vs pain ratio. The pleasure (if you're doing what you love) will always override the bad commentary you might receive and the risk of that happening.

When you enjoy what you do, that passion is contagious. You can see or feel it on screen when you watch a film or read a blog post and, of course, in person, when you meet someone who lives and breathes their art. It's like a magical force drawing you in.

Accept the internet for what it is

It's a platform where anything goes, literally. Embrace how bountiful and far-reaching it is and block or delete abusive comments, unsolicited advice and bitchiness.

Accept online life for what it is – at its best a supportive hub, but at worst a hellish place where trolls hide behind their screens. You are not in control of the world wide web, but you are in control of your response and your reaction to others. It's time to manage your emotions, to not entertain anything unreasonable and stay calm and strong.

Allow yourself to get upset

Don't squash feelings of sadness at comments and reactions to your work or yourself. Process them: talk, shout and cry if you need to. Distraction can be a great help, as can rooting yourself around those you love. Don't stop, though. You and your family depend on your job.

Of course, constructive criticism is vital and nourishing. If you agree on the comments made or can see the critic's point of view, make note, take action and improve. Meaningless bile, though, must be put on the 'crap pile' and disregarded.

Don't stop creating

When you read something that makes you want to stop and never write again, do the exact opposite. Do not stop creating based on someone else's subjective opinion of you or your work. Art is naturally subjective and divides opinion, and while as a personal brand it can be hard not to take criticism personally, channel negative energy into your work for positive results. Create. Write about criticism even.

Art heals, in so many ways and your story will no doubt help others.

Don't feed the trolls

Look, stick up for yourself, by all means, but equally know when to remain quiet. Drama with a capital D will diminish without fire and maintaining a dignified silence can be more powerful than responding.

Know yourself

When others condemn us, we often blame ourselves first. We question our work/online presence/looks/attitude/ (insert a million other things) when facing negativity, but it's crucial to remember that most people online don't know you as your friends and family do. There will always be envy alongside success, particularly in the competitive online world, and those green-eyed monsters really *can* be monsters, so don't take everything to heart.

Ultimately, know who you are, your strengths and, importantly, your flaws, so they can't be used against you. Keep that moral compass of yours pointed in the right direction and keep getting back up again and again.

Be kind

There's not enough kindness in the world. Try to always be kind, even to those who have hurt you.

When you are forced to work with someone who has caused you pain, do what Harriet Thrope advocates and, 'Disarm with charm' and, as my mum likes to remind me, 'Kill them with kindness'. People who dislike you will feel confused and bereft if you simply treat them with compassion. It's not easy, but it's possible, so put on a smile and be professional.

Count your blessings

We are incredibly lucky to be alive, well and able to write blogs, start businesses and work. Cherish these blessings. Do charity work and help others as a means to offer support and love to those who need it most. In doing so you also help yourself.

Have a digital detox

We all need time out – a chance to recalibrate and rest, ready to return with a clear mind. This might be switching off on evenings or weekends or taking a tech-free holiday. When things become too much, tune out.

KEEPING YOUR FIRE BURNING

Now, what happens if trolls, hyper-comparison or simply putting yourself out there drains the life out of you and makes you feel like you want to quit?

After a career break or maternity leave you might feel fuzzy or creatively blocked. Know, firstly, that you're not a machine, and it's normal to have periods when you simply lose your drive, especially after a hard knock, time away or negativity. It's hard not to take things personally when you're a personal brand. Being Marmite is better than being mediocre, right? Energy and time can be zapped when you've taken a bashing, so you must listen to your body and mind: rest, recuperate, then take some time to destress and return stronger than before.

Try not to put things off for too long though, as can be the case when you take a leave of absence. I like to take the pressure off when I'm returning to creative work after a short break or holiday by drawing, or making a film that I tell myself I don't have to share if I don't want to. Ease yourself in gently and, of course, start that way too. One post and film at a time.

If you do have a creative freeze then check out my tips to reignite your passion once more. Here's how to overcome a creative block:

Accept how you feel

Embrace your emotions, however silly or hard it seems. Be at peace with how you feel at this very moment. Trust it will pass. Similarly, with insomnia, if you lie there, anxious at the fact you're not sleeping, sleep will elude you. Accept that you can't sleep, practise meditation or deep breathing (I like to count the different sounds I can hear as a means of distraction), or get up and do something else before trying to sleep again – it works for me. The same applies to writer's or creative's block. Accept, distract, become active, and inspiration will come.

Talk about it. I find the greatest antidote to writer's block and the inevitable self-doubt that accompanies it, is to talk about it. Share your fears in order to process them and reduce their threat. Speak to those you trust, because once your worries are out there, they become less scary and easier to overcome. You'll also find comfort in other creatives admitting that they too suffer from blocks. Let's normalise creative's block in order to combat it more quickly.

Distraction is key

Distraction eventually leads to renewed inspiration and motivation. Go for a walk, hang out with people who make you laugh, and pursue something else creative. Change form and medium to switch things up: paint if you usually write, try your hand at poetry if you usually write prose, and vice versa. Pick up an instrument and expose yourself to other people's art too, visiting a gallery or museum, or watch content online you'd otherwise ignore. Open up your mind. Liberate yourself from the pressure to create and immerse yourself in something else. Remember that you have to *live* in order to *create*. Don't forget that, as with your other muscles, your creative muscles (arms and brain) need a break too. Don't beat yourself up about it. Everyone needs recovery time. The greatest athletes need to rest to win the race!

Do something different. I find that accomplishing something out of the ordinary, which pushes me out of my comfort zone, always gives me a confidence boost – be it starting Pilates or cooking something I've never made before. When you feel like you've lost your creative mojo, the fear can be overwhelming ... You question whether you'll ever write/film/paint again. Trust that when you love something, it will return. Passion always overrides fear. This current slump will pass.

Write daily at dawn

One of my most beloved books on writing is the classic *Becoming a Writer* by Dorothea Brande, written in 1934. Dorothea advocates writing as soon as you wake up, 'training yourself, in the twilight zone between sleep and the full waking state, simply to write'. Write a stream of consciousness, without judgement or rereading it, and before reading a paper or checking your phone. It will help free you from the pressures of writing with a purpose, rather than enjoying the act of writing. Thanks to this daily practice, you will rediscover the joy of simply writing for yourself and the pleasure of it, and before you know it, you will be sharing your work with the world once again.

BOOST YOUR CREATIVITY

I also want to share some creativity boosters that help me day to day. Sometimes we just need to encourage our creative muscles into action even when we least feel like it.

Discover your peak creative time

I'm a bit of a night owl, to be honest, and while I write, shoot and edit throughout the day, I love losing myself in my blog and book writing when the house is fast asleep and all is quiet. There are no distractions then, on- or offline, and having written for a lot of the day, my creative muscles are warmed up and ready for the night sprint. I feel that the magic hour of creativity happens for me when the moon emerges. It's when I create my best work. I'm most focused and committed then. It's also when the kids are fast asleep!

Do remember to switch off tech an hour or more before sleep, though, to rest your mind pre-slumber.

We all need a push when work life can feel lacking or stale

The more you write, the more you write, until the process is normalised and you create free-fall, overcoming self-doubt as confidence surges and creativity becomes your default mode. It's those times that you forget everything else and hone in on your art. It's magical.

Luckily, that's where I'm at most of the time – through dedication. We do all flounder and fall, though. It's part of the journey, and that's why we need to remind ourselves what works – the small triggers that boost our creativity and get us back on track.

Music

Music can stir, inspire and uplift. It can set your working ambience too. I would often play music relevant to the scenes in the screenplays I was writing in order to help set the tone for myself and my characters. Cypriot songs in particular, played while I wrote short films, would transport me to the world I was creating. Music is a powerful creative tool and it's one I return to time and time again.

Classical music is a tonic for the soul. I often play Classic FM in the morning to help ease me into the day. It's also the ideal way to eliminate school-run stress for all the family. If you find that music distracts you from the words on the page, try playing tracks before you start – perhaps in the car – selecting songs to suit your mood and the tone of your work.

Repetitive action

I find inspiration often strikes when I'm in the middle of a repetitive action, such as driving, running or ironing. I often conceive my best ideas on the treadmill. Don't switch off from driving to write down an idea of course (stay safe), but once you've pulled up, get it onto paper so you don't forget it. I like to write blog post titles of my ideas with a few notes alongside them so I remember to return and flesh them out at a later date. It helps me to be prolific. My house is full of notepads.

Time out

You are more productive when you rest, recover and relax. Working in overtired mode rarely creates the best results, and when we're all so busy juggling and hustling it's vital to take time out – even if that means just twenty minutes a day doing something unrelated to work that feeds your soul and restores your energy. Yoga, painting, a walk in the countryside, a manicure or some meditation using an app will allow you to produce better work when you return to getting your head down.

The arts

Take time to visit art galleries and the theatre, to read widely across all genres, and to enjoy the feel of books between your hands. Feel fully immersed in and inspired by the world around you, and on living life. Without experience you have nothing to write about.

Creative people

Surround yourself with other creatives: people who understand, stimulate and stretch you. Choose those who make you ask questions, critique your work and self-reflect, and who inspire you to bravely be yourself.

Chapter 5

MUM GUILT AND THE ART OF JUGGLING

So, you've decided to get back to work, whether that's from home or in the office, and sometimes life feels a little *rough* and everything's all too much. The ever-changing demands of family and professional lives don't always add up, and everyone is in pursuit of the mythical work–life balance, which doesn't really exist. The truth is, while you might be able to have it all, you generally can't have it all at the same time. So, how should we be rethinking the idea of 'balance' and applying it to our own lives? In this chapter, I share my thoughts on mastering the art of the juggle, learning to prioritise and how to co-parent successfully. I also take a look at splitting and managing the domestic workload, and creating a system at home that means, most of the time at least, you'll have some sort of harmony at work and at home.

The juggle is never easy. Not at all. Worth it? Yes. Easy? No. Having it all is a ludicrous concept and impossible really – not in the seamless, stress-free way we've been led to believe, thanks to the media and the myth of Supermum. We're all on this elusive search for balance – moderation, even – but that's the thing about moderation: you even need that moderately. Most of us want to raise a family and work too. Whilst running your own business can offer greater flexibility, it's no less time-consuming or stressful than a 'standard day job'. I've found it to be high maintenance, truth be told. Yes, you have more control over your schedule, but you're still completely overstretched (because there's never enough time, whatever you do), and the stakes are raised when you're self-employed as you're completely invested in your business and dependent on it to succeed.

Juggling work with family commitments and personal trauma while writing this book meant finding strength and resilience I didn't know I had. It's also reminded me about the importance of acceptance: coming to terms with what you cannot change, and leaning on art to help and heal. That's adulthood, and parenthood. Life with kids, work and responsibilities can be busy and overwhelming. You know that saying, 'You want something done, then give it to a busy person'? I'm that busy person and I'm often shattered! The thing is, however bad things get, however tough a day I might have, being with my kids uplifts me. There's no time to wallow with little ones and it helps that kids are hilarious.

Some days feel relentless. Somehow, though, I meet my deadlines, collect the kids from school and get a book written. It means lowering standards (if you could see my kitchen now – or my ironing pile), but that's balance and compromise and moderation. We are moderately calm here and moderately manic. The ironing pile is moderately ironed! You must accept that life will feel hectic when you're a mumboss.

This kind of candidness about self-employment often startles people. Being your own boss doesn't mean immediate or even consistent contentment, but no way of working can offer that. I do know for certain, though, that being my own boss works for my whole family overall. I feel stimulated when writing and directing on my own platforms. I find joy in meeting readers on the street and hearing about their own mumboss businesses. I love time off with my kids after school midweek, working when they sleep because I control my schedule. I've basically redefined balance. A late night writing this book is followed by a quieter day, heading to the park with the kids and hitting their homework before writing a blog post at night. That's how I usually roll.

Mumboss life will veer between self-congratulatory success when you feel you're winning in both spheres of your life, and the feeling of doom as you deem yourself a failure in both. The key is to adapt to the emotional ups and downs of work and mum-life by being kind to yourself on the tough days, and elated when you nail things on the good ones. If you're doing a job you adore, that will see you through the shizz for sure!

I know I'd rather feel stressed doing something I love, with glorious rewards both emotional and financial, than the alternative, wouldn't you?

HOW TO PRIORITISE

While so many of us have never had it so good working in the digital field, it's worth acknowledging how hard prioritising can be, especially when your to-do list features twenty emails to yourself, a Google calendar, a wall calendar and notes in biro on your hands. Guilty!

Writing this book has meant missing friends' birthdays and weekend breaks away, and not putting the kids to bed as frequently as I would like to. Yes, it's worth it in the long run, but it doesn't mean it's a walk in the park when I'm getting my head down. Missing out and guilt cut deep. Weigh up the sacrifices you're making, though, and be realistic. Real friends will understand if you can't attend a party. Send a present and make it up to them when you've met your deadline. You can't do and be everything so accept that now.

Remind yourself that if you didn't have a job you loved – a creative outlet – you wouldn't feel as happy overall. Feeding your soul to feed your kids is paramount. I crave intellectual stimulation so when I lack it, I'm a miserable mum – and who wants one of those? Give yourself permission to start something new or return to work if you want to or have to.

When it comes to the question of equilibrium, I'm reminded of the words that the priest on my wedding day wisely shared. He advised me that a long-lasting marriage is built on two people consistently compromising. I think a lot in life relies on compromise. No more so than life with kids. I compromised on my pre-baby flat stomach and it's been a running theme ever since. You don't need to compromise on your values now that you want to juggle work and a family, but understanding that no one finds the juggle easy is vital for your mental health. Many mums you see online might have additional help – nannies, cleaners or family on side to help with everything – and there's no shame in that either. This juggle helps me understand the pressures that other parents feel. It's given me a sharpened sense of clarity and empathy for others too. Becoming sensitive to my kids' needs has also made me more compassionate, which has helped in how I communicate with colleagues and in my approach to campaigns and collaborations. Being a mum helped me be a better boss!

PMT and menopausal expert and author Maryon Stewart (maryonstewart.com) feels the same. She shares that pregnancy, birth and having kids helped her to become more sensitive to her patients' needs:

'Pregnancy and breastfeeding together with the demands of a busy home life centred around children's needs (I had four), helped me to better understand the juggling act that the PMS patients in my clinic have to face. It gave me insights that only practical experience could, and allowed me to come up with tips and recommendations that were realistic. It also helped me to prioritise what was important so that I could be there for my patients at given times (unless of course an emergency cropped up like my son swallowing a one-pound coin!) as well as being there for my little ones, including never missing nursery or school concerts and events. I used some of my income to pay someone to do the jobs I didn't enjoy, resulting in time at home being fun play time which I looked forward to and enjoyed enormously.'

LETTING GO OF THE GUILT

The biggest conflict I often feel as a parent is the equal pull of wanting to be with my kids and to be working. I frequently have a simultaneous desire to do both. Guilt is a mother-f**ker. No one feels guilt like a mother. This is exacerbated by second-guessing yourself as a parent, when you endlessly question if your choices are the right ones. This, in turn, can lead to self-doubt in all areas of your life, including business. Plus, sep-aration anxiety affects both mother and child and, if you let it, guilt can grow and grow, feeding itself until it reaches monster proportions, killing the work-related elation you deserve to feel. Distraction is powerful, though – for both of you. There was many a morning over the years when I felt torn and teary-eyed dropping Alexander off at nursery. Looking into my eyes, he would pull at my heartstrings, appealing to leave so we could spend the day together. He would beg to be with me, 'Because

I love you Mummy'. The sweet goodbye handshake we would always do before kisses and cuddles often tipped me over the edge. I've lost count of the number of times I just wanted to scoop him up and run out of the nursery together. I would often sit in the car blubbing after drop-off because it felt so unnatural to leave him and head to work.

A call to the nursery five minutes later would always reassure me that he was happily running around with his pals in the playground, stimulated by the activities and camaraderie nursery provided him. By then, I too would have recovered from the intense emotion of the morning and, once immersed in the day-to-day mechanics and creative side of the business, the client calls, the creative briefs, the blog posts that would come from the heart (usually on topics just like this), I would feel OK again. Doing what you love helps you to overcome the guilt. That space away working would enable me to rationalise the situation. I would remind myself that I would be seeing my kids at the end of the day and that my job brings me great joy. Happy mum, happy kids, right?

Thanks to my flexible career, Alexander and I had, for the most part, at least one day, if not two, together during the week before he started school. Doing a job that excites me made leaving my child in nursery bearable. I also knew I'd have a full day or two with him soon after. Likewise, your job has to be worth the pain you might feel at times, the separation anxiety or missed milestones.

That doesn't mean I don't feel frazzled most days. I cried like a baby when I got the dates wrong for the Christmas Nativity and missed my eldest son's speaking part, but that's the compromise, isn't it? Not everything will run smoothly, and in general we're happy with our lot, our routine and our full and dynamic lives. I'm grateful too for the late starts and early finishes. For the many times that I'm able to make concerts, awards, school trips, bake sales and more. Being a blogger and vlogger offers my children greater stability (my directing job would have seen me travel solo and work twelve-hour days), as I'm present and proactive in their everyday lives.

DECIDE WHAT YOU WANT FROM WORK

If you're struggling for motivation or are just not sure about making the jump to going self-employed or returning to work full or part time (many don't have that choice – not immediately anyway), start making notes on what it is you want from your work life. On one side of a notepad write a list stating what your current situation is lacking, and on the other side, the steps you need to take towards achieving your 'new life'.

When I had Oliver, my first list would read:

- I need a creative space to call my own.
- I want to make meaningful connections with like-minded people.
- I want to feel like myself again.
- I want a job that works around my child.

My second list was:

- Try new things, start painting again. Start a blog or YouTube channel.
- Join social media and connect with other creative mums.
- Attend a blogging conference/event to learn and connect.
- Email established creatives for advice.
- Watch how-to videos on blogging and vlogging.

If you are employed, ask yourself these questions:

- Can you ask HR at work for a more flexible schedule?
- Could you start an e-business by night and at weekends, while you still work your day job?
- Could you juggle both?
- Can you take some time out or work during your maternity leave?
- Can your parents or friends help a day or more a week?

It might take a while to find your path. Over the years, I have done every job under the sun, from selling wine and working in restaurants to producing radio and presenting telly, writing screenplays and beyond, until finally finding what I'd been searching for: being a mum and writing and filming about it. It's my ideal job and isn't solely focused on parenting but also all of my loves: fashion, food, film and more. Becoming a mum of two made me focus on the skills I wanted to hone and made me determined to follow a creative job that I was in charge of. Motherhood made me a better writer because I had less time in which to write, so I made every word count. The huge spectrum of emotion I've experienced with motherhood has heightened my empathy and in turn my creativity and means of expression.

My friend Stacey Hirlam, an English teacher, found that although she was torn at first when it came to returning to work after kids, she too found that being a mum improved her work.

'Being a mum has helped me develop my role as a teacher and a form tutor because I have learnt how to empathise more with my pupils and understand their individual needs because no child is the same. For every pupil who is the star of the rugby team and achieving A grades in their exams, there is the pupil who has to metaphorically climb a mountain just to get into school on a morning. That mountain may be making breakfast for other siblings, caring for disabled parents or sometimes it's unimaginable. I wouldn't say I care more now I am a mum – I've always cared – but now I understand that things don't always run smoothly at home so if homework is regularly 'left at home' I find out why or if a child's behaviour and attitude change suddenly I investigate and we work through it. Being a mum is also a great ice breaker with a new GCSE class because everyone loves an exploding poo story – especially if the said poo may or may not have landed on their English teacher's face.'

Becoming a mum will serve and enhance your working life, even if it doesn't always seem that way initially.

SHARING THE PARENTING LOAD

Balance and guilt are, of course, inextricably linked. The guilt can be all-consuming, even for the most seemingly together of individuals. We're all eaten up by guilt and, unfortunately for many, support is often lacking or not seized on at work or at home.

Please don't feel you have to do it all, and do reach out for help. At home, can you ask your partner for more help? I couldn't do what I do without the physical and emotional support my husband Peter provides. He makes the packed lunches in the morning and we share the drop-off and collection of our kids at school, depending on my deadlines and when he needs to start work.

We have a housework rota, with the kids doing chores (cleaning their rooms, clearing the table, stacking the dishwasher), and we've divided tasks so Peter puts the clothes wash on and cleans the bathrooms, while I mostly iron and vacuum. We share the cooking equally as it's something we both love to do. We also have a cleaner once a week. All this keeps our home life ticking over so we can crack on with working from home.

Can you do the same? Are there family members who could give a hand? If you're a single parent or don't live near family, are there friends who can help or a support network you can reach out to locally? Single parent friends of mine take it in turn to look after one another's children while they work freelance, and also do car pools for drop-off and collection from school. Create a home-life schedule as you would a work one. Locate where you need extra help and divide responsibilities with your other half to help you as you start your own business or return to work. Could you too hire a cleaner and/or a babysitter to take up some of the slack? Can you work smarter, wake up before your family to blog or dedicate time at lunchtime? Are there pockets of time on your train commute or Sunday afternoons free you can use to catch up on work?

SPACE TO WORK FROM HOME

If you're working from home, create a space of your own to help you distinguish between the two spheres of your life. Here are some tips:

- Can you set up an office in the corner of your bedroom, or convert the spare room into a micro office? If, like me, you use your kitchen or dining table as your desk, can you hide away your computer and anything work related once the kids are back from school and you're making dinner or watching Netflix and chilling (not *that* Netflix and chilling)?
- Libraries are a lifesaver if I need to get out of my messy home

and into a calm space with my laptop in hand. I mostly opt for my local library, or I'll pop to the British Library if I'm in town.

- Cafes also hit the spot for refuelling while working. People-watching is good for the soul too and will help to inspire you. A change of scenery can be motivating so embrace your local options.
- It's normal to feel stuck in a work rut at home, especially when the washing, ironing and dirty dishes pile feels overwhelming, so when things feel too much, look outwards – can you work at a friend's place or look at studio- or desk-sharing with a like-minded creative to recharge your work life?
- Vitally, don't live to work. Take regular breaks, because working from home can mean that you never actually stop working. The days where I go for a run after school drop-off, and take time to ease into my day, end up being far more productive than diving headfirst into work. I also love getting fresh air on my lunch break. It clears the mind and is good for my health.
- Working remotely means being able to do business anywhere at all. You can type away from a sun lounger on holiday, or from your local Starbucks, so don't forget that. Working from home is convenient but in theory you can work wherever you like!
- Importantly, get organised – whether you're working from home or in a day job. Prioritise your work to-do list and remove on- and offline distractions. You do not need to watch that cat video on Facebook!

Ursula Tavender, my friend and blogger at Mumbelievable.com, a site that empowers mothers, advises you to:

'Get organised, and then put contingency plans in place so you can handle unexpected situations with confidence. If your work involves commitments it would be tough to get out of when your child is ill, for example, having a back-up childcare plan can remove stress and enable you to keep working. Just knowing you've considered the inevitable unforeseen scenarios can make returning much smoother.'

These are my working essentials:

- Laptop computer for writing, video and photo editing, emailing, social media and keeping up with the news
- iPhone/smartphone
- Portable battery (lifesaver on the road)
- Camera if vlogging/filming – I love my Canon G7X Mark II, which is lightweight, easy to use (shoot on auto if you like), creates quality images and works well for photos too with a flip screen
- Tripod for steady shots (I like Manfrotto)
- Sync work and home calendars – vital when it comes to handling a busy work and school calendar. I work as far in advance as I can
- Don't forget the snacks to keep your blood sugar level and your brain in gear

While working from home is the easy answer for us all, it does require some work to protect each role of mum and boss, so you have control over your work and home life. Serial entrepreneur, mum of four and former Dragon on *Dragons' Den*, Sarah Willingham offers advice on how to achieve this:

'Don't mix the two. When you're a mum be a mum and be present in the moment – don't feel guilty, just enjoy your time being a mum. Take time to do small things with the kids without going through lists of the 1000 things you still haven't done. Take your emails OFF your phone if you are like me and can't stop checking them. So, you only work when you actually sit down to work i.e. sit at your laptop.'

When I'm 'at work' at home, I'm open and honest with my kids that I'm currently writing or filming, so that they know what I'm doing and understand that this is 'Mummy's work time'. Even if I'm sitting beside them as I work, provided that they're happy and have what they need, I'm clear that, right now, I'm working so I can earn money to buy the things we need. Children are surprisingly logical for the most part; providing they are old enough to understand, you just need to explain what you are doing, and when, so they can respect the time you need to work.

We all make sacrifices when it comes to juggling kids and careers. It might be sleep or your favourite soap. While you might not be able to watch telly every night, make time for that movie one night a week, because 'all work and no play' will make you fall out of love with life and your business. It's vital throughout this balancing act, which is tough going, to look after yourself: eat well and exercise, and recognise the importance of sleep, which aids productivity.

An important note about style: this might sound frivolous, but what you wear has an impact on your mood and day. I'm far more productive if I change out of my 'good intention' gym kit, throw on a dress and a flick of eyeliner and set to work. Approach your home set-up as you would a business meeting. Make some effort. Obviously not every day – nobody's got time for that, and the beauty of working from home means you can stay in your PJs and no one need know it – but when it matters, get dressed up, even if it's just to make a deadline or take that work call that requires you to feel a little bit more powerful.

Finishing this book saw me don some MAC Lady Danger red lips, a tea dress and a power jacket for one last read through before I hit *send* to my editor. Boom. Clothes are another way to express yourself to the world. Get creative in all aspects of your life and it will show up on the page or at work. It helps you feel more professional, which filters into every aspect of your work life.

CHILDCARE

For those back at work, childcare is necessary to ensure that you can work either full or part time. We personally opted for nursery as we lived close to a super one, and we felt that the classroom environment, with lots of outside play overlooking the countryside, would appeal to our kids.

Meet childminders and visit nurseries so you can chat through your expectations and, as with everything, go with your gut. You know your child better than anyone else. Some children are better suited to a more intimate environment that a nanny or childminder can provide, while others prefer a more social environment at nursery.

When starting your own digital business, succeeding without childcare is, of course, possible. You just need to be time savvy and you will have to work on evenings or in pockets of the day when your baby or toddler naps. Alternatively, someone might be able to help out.

I have friends who work full time and rely on their own parents, along with their partners, to be flexible with start and end times at work, or they invest in after-school clubs as we do. Many say they're tired of trying to meet everyone's expectations – their kids' and their own – but ultimately feel the rewards at work are worthwhile. The feeling of independence, of financial security and doing a job they love, makes the daily battles (and often cheese and biscuits for dinner) a small compromise overall.

TIPS FOR HAPPY JUGGLING

Below are some quick-fire tips on how to handle the balancing act – from reaching out for support to meal planning and letting go of perfection. Whether you set up at home, or work nine to five, these ten tips will help empower you:

1. Let go of perfection. Lower your standards. I'm a clean freak, but I accept the house will be messy, and some things are more important than endless tidying. We do a big tidy most weekends, and while we clean throughout the week, we don't obsess about it. Let that shit go.

2. Co-parenting or reaching out for support from others will help you. Remember, getting downtime for yourself helps everyone. I love a blow dry to chill out and return bouncier. Split duties and create a rota to ensure all hands are on deck. The home doesn't have to be your sole responsibility, so stop trying to do everything.

3. Shop online so supermarket sweeps and extra spending are kept to a minimum. Look for deals, cook and freeze in bulk.

4. We sort the packed lunch my son takes to school the night before, making only the sandwiches fresh in the morning. This saves time and limits stress.

5. The same goes for clothes. I plan out the kids' clothes the night before, along with my own, as mornings are always manic. I also wash and iron uniforms at the weekend so there's always enough during the week.

6. After school, and on weekends, allow your kids to be bored. They must learn to use their imaginations. It's not your job to constantly entertain your kids. Do I look like Mr Tumble?

7. My children have been doing chores since they were small. Getting them involved in home life allows them to feel independent, and means they can contribute to tidying from an early age. My brother and I did this too as kids, and because of it, settled into university life away from home with ease. Start as you mean to go on.

8. Learn to switch off and allow yourself time out, and off. Yes, kids change you, but deep down you're still that same person; you just need to find yourself again, so give yourself permission to have fun. You don't need to be a martyr. Redefine the way you see motherhood. You don't need to stop being bold when it comes to style and beauty or have a personality transplant because you popped some kids out. Have fun nights out and enjoy the things you loved pre-kids when you can.

9. Try to carve out some couple time too, even if it's once a month. I love watching Netflix with my husband or going on a date night once a month, and remembering who we are and how much we love each other, away from the daily grind and bickering that comes with raising kids.

10. Get yoga into your life. It's transformed mine. I watch short YouTube videos and often do deep breathing from my desk. A total game changer when it comes to juggling. Get into the routine of practising on a Monday, which will encourage you to keep it up all week.

'You time' isn't selfish, it's necessary. The more time you have for yourself, the more mental capacity you have for both your family and your business.

Chapter 6

BLOGGING, VLOGGING AND BUILDING AN ONLINE BUSINESS

Although this chapter focuses on building your own business, these rules can also apply if you are going back to a career, as they will help you to return to work even better than before. I have lots of friends who use blogging and vlogging as a creative outlet outside of their day jobs. Blogs and vlogs are for everyone!

I feel grateful for my blog and the platform that the internet has given me and millions of others. We have everything we need at our fingertips. There is no excuse not to act. You and your laptop can achieve whatever you work for. As Seth Godin, global thought leader and bestselling author of *Purple Cow*, *Linchpin* and *Tribe*, so wisely stated when I interviewed him on the blog, what the internet gives us is:

'Leverage. All the tools we used to have to build ourselves are there, for anyone to use. You have the same access as a billion-dollar corporation. You can use them or not, but we can't deny that the access is there.'

In this chapter, I want to start with my story of going from zero to hero (!), aka nought to six figures plus. I also include tech tips and advice on how to manage your finances so you can develop your personal brand and shine online. I know discussing money is not a very British thing to do, but let's unstiffen those upper lips for a moment and focus on how to make a living doing what you love. I want to celebrate the fact that in these digital times, our art – words, opinions, videos and distinctive selves – can translate into money. A lot of money. It simply takes some self-belief (even if it's feigned at first) along with a commitment to honing your craft, and then crafting consistently.

Just start. Now.

Making that first step to launching a blog is a huge milestone. You will provide yourself with a space that you control and own – or at least hire (rent-free), if you're working on YouTube, for example. Author of *The Million Dollar Blog* book Natasha Courtenay-Smith agrees:

'What is clear is that no successful blogger of the 50 or so I talked to for the book [*Million Dollar Blog*] knew all the answers before they started. You learn as you go along, but you can't begin to learn until you start.'

You can write and publish whenever you like, and as the internet reflects its users, there is someone for everyone. A live medium, it will grow with you and reflect your own personal growth and ever-changing interests. In the early days, I focused on sharing the funny side of parenting (it was my way of surviving the harder times), but my content evolved as I did, and began reflecting my growing interests.

We now find ourselves in a time where brands are focused on the power of digital influencers. A study by Nielsen from 2016 suggests that advertisers see an eleven times higher return on investment from influencer marketing as compared to traditional digital marketing. There is so much trust there, because online creators are seen as 'real' celebrities – people who feel like they're your friends. I am always amazed to be recognised by readers on the street in the UK, and even abroad, but reach is reach, and it's powerful.

Now is the ideal time to begin your blogging career. Blogging and vlogging are viable careers that can be built quickly with dedication and regular content. As an established blogger and vlogger, I have learnt along the way, making mistakes and learning from them so you don't have to. You can just begin writing online, and by utilising the wealth of knowledge that's already there on what works best, meet milestones quickly.

You might well feel confused and unsure about what it is you want to do: a blog, vlog or business, so ask yourself . . .

What do you enjoy reading and watching yourself? Do you love to watch YouTube videos on repeat, or is the written word more your thing? Do you like to draw/sew/source products? Then perhaps an e-shop is for you. Think back to what made you tick pre-kids, or even as far back as when you were a child yourself. What brought you joy? If you could change your life and career, what would you do? Know that it's still within your grasp.

Now is the perfect opportunity to do anything you wish, and to build on that. You don't have to choose one single thing either. I enjoy filmmaking as much as writing so I blog and vlog. I adore fashion and beauty and hope to bring out my own clothes and make-up line one day.

Stop limiting yourself and seize this digital space.

VLOGGING FOR BEGINNERS

Once you establish what burns a fire within, you can start your new business, and life.

Whatever you do, consider picking up a camera to promote yourself and your business.

It is estimated that over half of all internet video traffic will be content-delivery traffic by 2019. Brands and viewers flock to video for real personalities and powerful, engaging content. Video forms the majority of my own work and this will only continue.

Here I share my tips to help you vlog and go live on platforms such as Facebook and Instagram with confidence:

We all feel self-conscious on camera – just go for it

The more you do it, the less of a big deal it becomes and the easier it is to watch yourself! I always feel nervous before I go live, particularly as Facebook counts you in beforehand, but those nerves *spur me on*. You need that little pump of adrenaline to help you *go, go, go*! Plus, like anything, the more you do it, the easier it becomes. Give your creative muscles a workout.

When I decided to vlog more regularly over on YouTube, I forced myself to do it daily for months. Now I usually only make one video a week, but that period of simply cracking on every single day, even on the most mundane of days, means that self-shooting has become second nature to me. Yes, I worked in TV and film in my former life – and have loved being on camera since I was a child – but I still felt I needed greater practice in front of the camera. It gave me a boost, and it will you.

I'm now comfortable to vlog or go live anywhere, anytime. I never feel self-conscious and I'll happily seize opportunities for Facebook and Instagram lives. I've filmed 'live' with Jamie Oliver, Aldo Zilli, Emma Bunton and more. I love the thrill of 'going live'.

What should you shoot?

The age-old question of what to shoot is one I'm asked all the time. I say, shoot what you'd want to see yourself. I love a bit of reality TV: it makes me happy to shoot family parties, my dad making pancakes or being silly, or the self-help content which reflects my blog and purpose. And that's the thing: you're meant to enjoy what you do, and your viewers can tell if you're having fun or not. Passion is infectious – and watchable. It's hard not to reciprocate a smile when someone smiles at you. Watching those who love what they do is enticing and engaging.

If you give it a real shot and still hate being on camera, then don't sweat it – it's not for everyone. Just give it a chance (I would recommend several weeks of constant filming, even if you don't publish what you shoot) before you throw the towel in – and even then, take a break and give it another go before you abandon it forever.

Don't forget, too, when it comes to content – as with your site and other social media – a like-minded audience will always find you. If you want to shoot videos of cats all day long, or focus on beauty hauls, then cat and beauty lovers respectively will find and watch you.

Just be yourself

Be inspired by others, of course, that's necessary (we don't live in a vacuum), but always be yourself – unapologetically you. Believe me, folks can tell a mile off those who are genuine and, honestly, that transparency is worth more than anything in these crazy times we live in. We all want to follow people we trust. Eliciting trust and innovating is what you need. If you are approached to work on a campaign, value your voice and perspective on things, and speak up, suggesting ways of working that would resonate with your audience. You know your audience best. That's exactly why bloggers and vloggers are taking over the world and rivalling traditional media and many multi-media brands.

What kit do I need?

Your phone and an easy-to-use camera with some editing kit are all you need. You don't even need to edit when you film Facebook lives: you go live, then hit finish and publish if you choose to. (People will have watched it in real time but you can discard it after that if you prefer.) You don't have to invest in anything more than a phone either. I use an iPhone 6s for lives and my Canon G7X Mark II for vlogging and videos. My husband and I share a Canon 5D too if we do multiple camera set-ups or for photography, but the G7X offers pro quality for either too. I like my extendable Manfrotto tripod. When it comes to editing, there are lots of in-phone editing apps like iMovie (Apple), Adobe Premier and CyberLink (PowerDirector), which you can also use on your computer.

Professional YouTube creators share their tips and tutorials on the platform and the YouTube Creator Academy is a fountain of knowledge so check them out, too. Always customise your images on YouTube and Facebook, adding subtitles too, as most viewers watch online content with subtitles (I like the very reasonable rev.com). Also make sure you create SEO (search engine optimisation)-worthy titles (see page 190 for more on SEO) and put a description box, along with a link to your blog, in the description box and social media urls.

Which platform should I use?

Use as many as you fancy. I tend to stick to Facebook Live, and going live on Instagram, and I upload videos to YouTube and natively (shared directly) on Facebook, as well as stories on Instagram, too. I like to mix things up on YouTube, as with my website, and flit between my interests there, with my car videos proving most popular. It's often the mother in the family who decides which car to buy. YouTube, like your blog, relies on SEO as well as regular viewers/subscribers.

CREATE A PERSONAL BRAND

You need to do it your way. Yes, that sounds cheesy, but it's true. Be yourself, because that's what people want to see: a person who speaks the truth, whom they can trust and who feels like a friend. They will watch, read and keep coming back to your work because of you. It's as simple as that.

Know what you stand for, what your values are, and be consistent about them. Think of that person you know in real life (we all know one) who appears fake and insincere. They're not sure of themselves, so are trying to be someone they're not, turning everyone off in the process. Don't be that person.

Write about all aspects of your life and remember that life and interests evolve, so a lifestyle site gives you the space and freedom to grow and change.

Having various topics you cover enables you to reach more brands and garner greater and more varied opportunities. I have always simply been myself, sharing more and more of my life online as the years go on. I don't reveal anything that makes myself or my friends and family uncomfortable, and some things are sacred of course, but I do unflinchingly share what matters to me, both the good and the bad.

My goal is to help others, whether that's by sharing my stretch-marked tummy in a bikini or giving others hope that having a happy C-section after a horrendous one is possible.

Blogging and social media is a two-way street: my readers help, inform and support me as much as I do them. Social media is often a real-time conversation (particularly Facebook Lives), an online discourse that connects and, in many cases, transforms both myself and my viewer. People have kindly told me that my posts on blogging as a career have changed their lives. What a feeling! Being real, human, flawed and open is what generates a true connection between you, the creator, and the recipient. It's a connection based on respect, trust and camaraderie. A huge contributing factor to my success is that I'm told I'm warm and genuine online; that I draw people in.

So, how do you share who you are with the world and build a personal brand?

Salma Shah, personal branding psychologist, career coach and mentor (salmashah.com) shares her brilliant advice:

'Your personal brand is how people already describe you in a few words and, more importantly, it's that gut visceral deep-down feeling others experience in your presence or when they come across you online. The way you look, sound and behave all trigger powerful conscious and subconscious feelings.

Having a distinctive personal brand is like wearing your head-turning "LBD" (little black dress) with the perfect accessories that get you noticed for all the right reasons. There are millions of ways of pulling an outfit together but the way you wear that perfect LBD makes you distinctive, stand out from the crowd and is the ultimate crowd-puller. Not just any crowd but your audience.

A great website, Instagram feed, Facebook page with hustle and hard work will build your profile and get you attention. But to build a longer-term, powerful personal brand you need to connect with your audience or target market and go a lot deeper. For instance, there is no point having a tagline that says you 'serve others' when, once your audience starts to have a deeper connection with you, it becomes blatantly obvious that the only person you truly serve is yourself. The point here is if you are truly committed to raising your profile, and are in it for the long game, you need to be authentic in order to succeed.'

THE RECIPE FOR ONLINE SUCCESS

Content is king

Content is king or, as I like to say, 'queen'. Write, write and write some more. Read widely, take writing and journalism courses, and keep applying and growing in all that you do, be it creating distinctive captions on social media, or making vlogs or Facebook lives that inform and entertain.

I tried my hand at many things while studying for my BA, and then MA, at Goldsmiths, University of London. Every holiday and weekend saw me gain placements in radio, telly, in magazines and even on an internet show – when only three people in the US used the internet. I got myself out there, I experienced what the media had to offer and learnt what made me happy. Studying screenwriting and direction led to a film-making career and meant I could work across lots of creative areas while driving and protecting the creative vision of each project.

Now, as a blogger and vlogger, I do the same. I'm selective about the brands I work with, collaborating with them on creative ideas, and retaining my personality in all that I do. Remember that you are being hired for your voice, visuals and take on things. Plus, you don't need huge audiences to earn either. Small, targeted audiences are vital to brands too and everyone starts small, remember.

Ideas are the lifeblood of a creative's work, so keep coming up with them and don't be precious if they're not greenlit. Nothing is ever wasted, and an idea not used for one campaign can be used for another. Never feel you have nothing to offer – make notes, conceive ideas and pitch to PRs and brands. You can Google 'PR' and the name of a brand to find a contact or go via Twitter or social media. Opportunity favours the bold! There is room for all online.

Break the 'rules'

Rules, rules, rules. A long list of rules appear to apply when it comes to creativity, but blogging and vlogging seem to be forms that break all the traditional rules and are leading the way. Learn the necessary rules: how to write engaging material and how to shoot – you need the basics, everyone does – but here's the exciting bit. Once you feel proficient, go ahead and break the rules (though not the rules of the social media platforms – don't cheat!), experiment, add your own flair and be fearless! The following tips will help:

Write for whomever you like

Yep, I get it, we have an audience that matters (use Google Analytics to get to grips with your demographic), but don't get obsessed with stats. My audience, in my head, when I write every single post, even now, is exactly the same as it was on day one: my mum and immediate family.

Being *you* is why people come to your site. It's that feeling your regulars get – the ones who adore and find you wise/funny/witty or whatever – when they visit your corner of the world, which brings the boys/girls/grannies to your yard. Remember that, when the doubt creeps in, and you start over-thinking your audience.

Blogging attracts like-minded people to your site, the majority via SEO, and then, of course, all those fabulous hard-earned followers: family, friends, social media-likers and people behind their laptops all over the world.

You don't need a niche

I've said it before – you are your niche! Look, I'm a writer, a shaker and a procreator ... I'm a million different things: I love European cinema as much as reality TV, adore Michelin-starred restaurants as much as McDonalds, flip between Margaret Atwood and Celia Ahern, I'm gluten free during the week but eat lots of bread on cheat day (despite the tummy ache). I'm as complex as you are.

And guess what, I write about what I care about and anything I fancy on that day/week/month. Yes, I run my blog as a magazine, I vary my posts and mix things up, but they always reflect my mood and who I am, as your blog will represent you.

By the way, do go ahead and only write in one niche if you choose to, but never feel restricted, compartmentalised or pigeon-holed (by yourself or others), or that you can't be free to write anything you like. If you're interested in something, then get blogging.

Be a bit pushy

Yes, pushy can be annoying, but the internet is a big place and you want and need to be heard/seen/discovered, so you need PR to publicise yourself.

Don't bother people, or relentlessly email contacts, but do

contact creatives who might be able to help promote your blog. If you were at a networking party, you'd seek out those who might be able to help you by offering you work or propelling you forward. Approach the online world in the same way. Reach out, email, tweet. The more you do it, the more confident you will feel about it and your work. It's time to grow a thick skin (more on that later).

Post as many times as you wish

Look, this is your blog, your time, your terms. I go live five times a day some days. There are no rules!

I balance personal posts with advertorials (writing engaging, paid-for posts on products and services I use and would recommend to friends), and my core material is based on our experiences as a family, opinion pieces and recipes.

The ideal is to blog twice or more a week so search engines like Google and your readers can expect regular and high-quality content from you. Similarly, YouTubers tend to create a new video twice a week, on a Wednesday or Sunday for example. Try to build your schedule for yourself.

Switch off

I'm paid to offer social media packages to clients, but I'm not always switched on. I don't look at my phone much over weekends, and I like to switch off for the majority of holidays and evenings, using SocialOomph for when I'm not online to tweet urls of posts. I don't want to constantly be connected to my computer, but I do try to reply to every single comment I receive on my blog and social media accounts – not always immediately, but when I can. That engagement is crucial. Respect your audience and those who have taken time to connect with you.

Think about what you hope to achieve, rather than how much you feel you should be on social media (maybe try to reply to comments on existing posts/tweets above writing lots of new updates), and dedicate time to incredibly fun and fruitful sites like Pinterest and Instagram.

Pinterest is my happy place online, it's so intimate and inspiring there, and it's a brilliant traffic driver to the blog too. You can schedule pins via Tailwind to help save time and generate clicks to your blog.

My routine after blogging is this

Submit the url to a search console as recommended by Nic Tuxford, senior project manager at digital marketing agency Exposure Ninja (exposureninja.com): google.com/webmasters/ tools/submit_url. This can help get your pages indexed quicker. Google has a 'crawl budget' so manually submitting can help. I share urls on Google Plus (with an image) and LinkedIn (focusing on content I think a business/professional audience will like), Facebook (both personal and blog pages and on my Honest Mum group). I pin images from my post to Pinterest, share an image on Instagram promoting the post and on Instagram Stories, and schedule tweets via SocialOomph on Twitter and pins via Tailwind. I use the App Preview to get an overview of my Instagram gallery before I post there too.

Get busy people!

KNOW YOUR WORTH AND WHAT TO CHARGE

Having a stellar manager can be invaluable. They can help open new doors by elevating your brand power, counsel you and help you to achieve your long-term goals while staying focused on market trends. However, a manager usually comes after you have built up your brand.

I didn't have a manager for a number of years, but the fact that I had been a TV and commercials director, pre-blogging, meant that I was both business savvy and experienced (I'd had an agent as a screenwriter and director), and had some idea of the market I was now working in. Plus, I was a dab hand at negotiation, after years of pitching for jobs. Handling commercial budgets and being aware of rates for creatives helped me to position myself professionally, as a blogger, from the start.

Rates and ranking

You don't need a media background to negotiate, but take note of the following. When you are asked for your rates, throw the question back at the client, asking what their budget is and the fee they had in mind for the brief. Negotiate from that place, knowing they've most likely gone lower than the budget they have. Don't play hardball too much, though, and overprice yourself. Remember that some projects are worth doing for experience, or in return for PR. While those don't pay the bills, they can help you accumulate experience, and the perception you are creating around your brand will make you more employable in the long run. At the start, relish opportunities where you learn – we all need to grow in order to progress – but don't make a habit of working for experience only. And don't do much work for free, as you must value your time. When I started out, I used my daily rate as a freelance director as a rough guide, comparing how that related to what I was being asked to do as a blogger and vlogger.

There are many variables when it comes to fees and budgets for each campaign, but I advise that you focus first on the platform you own: your blog and growing that space that you control.

Tim Cameron-Kitchen is the UK's bestselling digital marketing author, the head ninja at digital marketing agency Exposure Ninja (exposureninja.com), and host of the Exposure Ninja Digital Marketing podcast. He emphasises the importance of search engine optimisation (SEO) and boosting your domain authority (DA) and page authority (PA) to build authority and get the deals. As Tim explains, domain authority is a representation of a site's authority – the higher a website's DA, the more likely it is to rank. Domain authority is increased by acquiring backlinks (these link back to your blog, so in my case, honestmum.com) from other websites – and the higher the DA of those referral sites, the more their links will increase your own site's DA. Page authority represents a specific website *page's* authority, calculated in the same way – it depends on the authority and quality of links that point back to that particular page. Tim elaborates on why authority matters:

'Optimising your blog to increase its ranking on Google means that it brings in more visitors, which in turn makes it more attractive to brands looking for exposure to large audiences. When we're working with brands to identify bloggers who would make good partners, one of the key metrics we'll use is Domain Authority (DA), which is a measure of how authoritative your site is from a search engine's point of view, so there is a direct correlation between a blog's SEO and its earning potential.'

The greater the number of authoritative sites linking back to you, the higher you rank in search engines. It's a bit like influential friends in real life recommending you to others. Google and others trust what high-ranking sites tell them about others.

You can measure your domain authority and page authority to see how search engines view you. Use Moz to check this:

moz.com/researchtools/ose/. PRs will also look at this, as well as using their own tools to measure authority, engagement, quality and resonance.

Don't get bogged down by the numbers, though. We all start with one follower or a handful if we're lucky. That one person will, of course, soon become two, and they'll tell their friends, share your work online and, before you know it, people all over the world will be reading and watching your posts and video.

Now, while brands appreciate solid numbers across all platforms – blog and social – do not dismiss your blog. It could be your empire. The fees you can command for video and blog posts on your self-hosted site can easily surpass other platforms, so keep things in perspective. Focus on watering the fruits in your own garden, as I like to say, and keeping an eye on everything else.

Strong content is the name of the game.

GET REHIRED

Once you start doing work with brands, these are my tips for getting repeat work.

Create a media kit

This is a selling document detailing your work. Mine can be found on my Work with Honest Mum page (create one of those for yourself too): honestmum.com/work-with-me/. This includes my reach, work, latest campaigns and press, and sometimes a quote from a PR. It never includes a rate card, because each campaign varies depending on the brief. Negotiate on a brief-per-brief basis. My media kit includes vibrant, engaging photos, social media numbers, logos of clients and press I've collaborated with. It's updated monthly and *means business!*

Deliver on time

If you can't deliver promptly, be clear why and don't make a habit of it. PRs need dependable creatives. Make deadlines and be trustworthy.

Create impactful content

Produce professional, well-written content – ideally, with visually appealing photography and video that is engaging.

Over-deliver

Always go the extra mile so the PR or client appreciates your work. I over-deliver on every campaign, be it extra tweets/photos/hosting a competition etc.

Remind PRs of your work, regularly

PRs managing brand accounts will be working with a wide range of creatives on diverse campaigns for a whole roster of clients, so once a month, reach out to those you've worked with in the past, asking to be considered for upcoming campaigns. Attach your media kit and any recent press to the email too. Keep the email short, sweet and to the point – with your contact details visible at the bottom – and send away. Don't be afraid to be proactive. The early bird catches the worm, and new campaigns come in all the time. Don't badger, but remind others of your work – and that includes journalists, TV producers and anyone who might want to hire you or offer you PR.

Access your vital statistics

Most PRs will ask for insights or stats on campaigns, so learn how to collate Google Analytics and screenshot insights from Facebook, Instagram and Twitter. Once you're hired, you're accountable. Becoming familiar with statistical tools will offer insight into your demographic: who is consuming your work, from which country, gender and for how long.

Up your rates

As you grow, it's reasonable to increase your rates. With a higher profile and greater interest come bigger pay cheques.

NETWORKING, ON- AND OFFLINE

Talk to the press

Twitter is a great way to connect with journalists, who can be found via the #journorequest hashtag. The press needs stories, so don't be afraid to approach it with angles. Also use SocialOomph or a similar tool to schedule posts on the platform, driving traffic to your evergreen material there, and on YouTube or any other platform you want to promote. Facebook and YouTube are in competition so always upload videos natively on Facebook. Never simply link to a YouTube url, as its reach will be limited. Every social media handle is a business and they don't want to promote competing handles (Facebook owns Instagram, though) or have you 'bounce off' their platform elsewhere.

Mingle

Don't forget that you embody and represent your brand. You can get reasonably priced but professional-looking business cards made online (I like moo.com). Consider putting a photo of your face on them. Attend events, networking sessions, screenings and creative meet-ups to connect with like-minded mumbosses. Pack your business cards with you and get mingling. And don't forget to follow up on any connections made.

Run competitions

Blog competitions which run on your site help encourage traffic and enable you to reach a wider audience. I use the competition widget Rafflecopter (rafflecopter.com), where you can insert the details of your competition and be provided with the html code to run it on your site. You can ask entries to sign up to your newsletter, visit your Facebook page and more. Once live, I promote competitions on competition forums and blogs including the following sites:

PrizeFinder: theprizefinder.com
Loquax: loquax.co.uk
Competition Database: competitiondatabase.co.uk
Super Lucky: superlucky.me

I also run Follow and RT (retweet) competitions on Twitter for brands that are hugely successful, particularly when it comes to gift cards and chocolate (something everyone seems to love). Word of warning: do check with each individual social platform on what its competition policy is. Like and Share competitions on Facebook are prohibited, for example.

Link to others

Start a linky. A linky is a post on your blog where you include code that enables other bloggers and vloggers to link their own blog posts/videos to yours. This creates a blogging/vlogging 'party' where creatives connect (usually at the same time each week – with my own #Brilliantblogposts linky, it's a Wednesday pm), encouraging engagement/views and PR for their own work and yours. Sharing your space offers a platform others can use, helping promote your blog too.

The same applies to groups on Facebook. Start a group where others can promote their work and share your own content too, so that you all benefit from new connections, as well as the PR and visibility the group provides. Linkys and groups are a virtual way to network. Utilise these tools.

Mailing lists

Encourage readers and followers to subscribe to your blog (I include a widget above the fold of my blog in a prominent position to encourage sign-ups), and create daily, weekly or monthly newsletters to entice readers to click through and read your content. Those email addresses are gold dust, because they allow you to instantly connect to your fan/reader base. Never spam people, though. Respect your readers. Also, make sure you are aware of the latest regulations on data protection, as the law on the processing and storage of personal data is changing.

GETTING INVESTORS ON BOARD

If you are launching a business, you might need to seek financial support to make it work. The free app Mush (letsmush.com), set up by Katie Massie-Taylor and Sarah Hesz to help connect mums with children of the same age, raised £3 million in investment. Katie shares this advice about getting funding for your business:

> 'Finding angel investors is a bit of luck and a lot of introductions. There are some angel networks (made up of individual investors) that go through rigorous pitching processes. Search online for these. But there are a lot of people willing to part with £5,000–£15,000 on the back of a good idea – there are tax breaks in the UK for backing early stage businesses. So, tapping into these people and presenting the idea was what we did! Introductions are (and remain) a domino effect – one always leads to another. Only one or two meetings of the thirty we took were a waste of our time, the rest either led to investments or introduced us on elsewhere. To get started, we trawled LinkedIn for existing connections in that world.'

HANDLING YOUR ACCOUNTS

Once you're trading, you will need an accountant. Raj Dhokia founded the firm Kona Seven (konaseven.uk), which specialises in accounting and consulting services to the creative industries, including bloggers, vloggers, designers, movie makers, content creators and many more. Here I share Raj's wisdom on everything you need to know about handling your finances.

Ways to trade

Your business could be one of the following:

- sole trader
- limited company
- partnership
- community interest company
- charity

Small businesses are usually either a sole trader or a limited company, and it's important to choose the right one for you. Raj explains the difference:

> 'As a Sole Trader you are self-employed and you ARE your company. Your money is yours and you can spend it as you wish. All expenses come out of the same pot. As a Limited Company you work FOR your company. Any money you make, belongs to the company and you can pay yourself as an employee and shareholder.'

Raj usually recommends becoming a limited company due to the security and safety it offers. He urges you to always seek professional advice when making this decision and to use HMRC's website to understand the differences. I personally like being a director of my own company at Honestmum Limited, and while it means greater responsibility and work, the security aspect outweighs this.

What about taxes?

If you were to set up as a limited company, the company must pay corporation tax, which is set at 19 per cent, but changes year to year, meaning you must check the HMRC website. In contrast to income tax for sole traders, companies don't get a tax free allowance: corporation tax is paid on all profit, even one pound. However, Raj explains, this doesn't mean that having a limited company means you miss out on the £11,500 tax free allowance that individuals get. You would pay yourself a wage from your limited company as an employee and use up that tax-free allowance. Also, there are other tax reliefs available to companies not available to sole traders, which can help reduce your tax bill. Each circumstance is different and Raj advises that you always speak to an accountant to see what is best for you.

Liability

This is a big one, according to Raj. As a sole trader you are your company, which means if anything goes wrong, you could lose everything. As a limited company, however, you can only lose what belongs to the company, and therefore only anything you have put into it, or that it owns. Raj recommends that everyone should have insurance, which should cover you to an extent. However, as many clients are increasingly working in the fast-growing 'gig economy', creating uncertainty over the outcome of possible legal disputes, he recommends the extra protection of a limited company: 'To be blunt, if you were to get sued and lose, as a sole trader you could lose your house; as a limited company you generally wouldn't.'

Size

As you grow, being a limited company has its benefits. The admin when hiring staff is far simpler when you're a limited company, and separating costs is easier. With published accounts and regular updates, investors are more likely to look at you and value your business, without the need to filter out the personal cost. Also, if they want a 'piece' of the company, you would need the shares that come with a limited company. Some clients also demand that a company is limited, as company directors are held accountable for their actions, and it also reassures them that they are working with a legitimate company and not a hobbyist.

How to keep on top of your accounts as you grow

Admin can be tough when you have a busy business. Bookkeeping, compiling accounts and paying the right taxes at the right time takes time, energy and consistency. All of this can be managed by an organised and informed director. Raj advises reading the material on the HMRC website and various blogs and info sites. He gives a lot of information to his prospective clients, because it is always good for a business owner to understand their financial and legal obligations. However, he also knows that many businesses don't have the time for admin, or to understand their accounts in depth. Many clients just want to know their tax bills and when they need to be paid, and he handles the rest while offering insight into each quarter and which work was most profitable.

If you're DIY-ing it, Raj's tips below will make handling your accounts easier:

- Get a separate bank account.
- Use a program or spreadsheet to track business income and expenses.
- File your receipts into relevant months – using either envelopes or an index card box and separators.
- Know the dates when you need to send what to HMRC.
- Don't be scared to call an accountant or HMRC.

- Find an accountant who understands what you do and who you are happy having a regular conversation with.
- Understand what does and doesn't count as a business expense.

The implications of hiring staff – part time and then on payroll

You can employ others in the following capacities:

- internships
- part time
- full time
- freelance

There are financial implications to each method and different tax treatments. Generally, interns should be paid a nominal minimum wage and expenses through payroll. Part-time staff need to be on your payroll, and paid through your payroll for their time. Full-time staff work the full hours available, and have a full salary and benefits. When it comes to part-time and full-time staff, an employer must also provide a pension scheme. Many people work as freelancers now, and are paid an invoice at a set rate and amount (which is how I work with people in my business). These payments don't go through payroll and count as a cost to the business. It's usually easier and simpler to hire freelancers before moving to part- or full-time staff when you're ready.

The benefits of trademarking your brand

Trademarking is a method of protecting your business name. It is easy, has some cost attached and makes a statement about your brand. Both Honest Mum and Mumboss are trademarked in the UK. As reputation and brands grow, the identity needs to be protected by a trademark. Verification ticks on social media also protect against fraud and prevent others posing as you online. ·

Becoming VAT registered

Value added tax (VAT) is a tax on goods and services by HMRC. We pay VAT on most things, and when you're a business, you can charge VAT if registered. When your company makes £82,000 in revenue, it has to register for VAT. However, you can register for VAT before this if you think it will be useful for your business. Currently the general VAT rate is 20 per cent. It's best to speak to a professional, but in general – if you have a lot of expenses that include VAT – do consider registering. You must consider that if you want to claim VAT back from HMRC, then you must also charge it to your clients so that this balances out into a payment to you or to HMRC. There are other set-ups for VAT, but Raj's advice is to speak to a professional about it.

Becoming VAT registered takes more admin and time, but if you must do it, it quickly becomes routine and your accountant can help you manage it and be organised.

There you have it: the nuts and bolts of running a business in a financially sound and law-abiding way.

Chapter 7

HOW TO BE YOUR OWN BEST PUBLICIST

P R is crucial to success, whether you're a blogger, vlogger, business owner or all three. PR helps you to get your work and business 'out there' and you seen as an authority in your field – someone to be listened to and trusted. It doesn't matter how incredible your work is, if no one knows about it – or indeed, you – how can they watch, read and buy from you? This chapter will give you the know-how to promote your work and brand with ease.

Luckily, working digitally means you have everything you need to promote yourself, at the touch of a button, from organic SEO to targeted social media ads.

I realise that, for some, promoting your work might feel a little odd, unnatural or boastful even, but you must put those fears aside and establish a gallant attitude towards representing and promoting your business. The quicker you become accustomed to PR, speaking about yourself online and to press, and marketing what you do, the sooner you will find success. Using social media and a blog or YouTube channel as your platform, anyone can create, share and grow.

Stop being scared to self-promote. If you don't, you can't survive.

PR helps your visibility and reach. In simple terms, PR informs people about who you are, your personal brand and what you're selling. It might be a Facebook ad boosting your post or page or a local magazine featuring a piece on your site. It could even be a global brand, sharing your film for millions to see.

I've always been naturally good at PR. I certainly learnt from the best: my dad, 'Papa G', an entrepreneur who has been drumming the importance of PR into me since I was a kid. One distinct memory is him sharing marketing lessons with me as a teen when he was doing an MBA, and I would test him on what he'd learnt. Standing out from the crowd, finding story angles to your work/business/brand and reaching out to the press gate-keepers were just a few key lessons my father taught me. And they stuck.

Dad even encouraged me to print out my CV, roll it up and put it into a glass bottle, rather than submit the usual CV with letter, when I was seeking work experience in TV and radio aged sixteen. He wanted me to stand out from the crowd (everyone in my class in this case) and it worked. The work experience was secured. My dad is so sentimental that he kept every letter I ever sent to media companies over the years in a file in his office titled 'Vicki' – to remind me of my tenacity and journey.

Thinking outside the box became the norm for me. I would look at how most people were creating and presenting their work and I'd experiment with five different ways of doing it, until I found something unusual about my story.

I would always treat everyone I met on my journey with respect and uphold the view that everyone could teach me something new, even those I least expected to. This ethos was inspired by my parents. It was the innovative, fearless, but always generous way that my dad did business that rubbed off on me. He was never ruthless – nor am I – but passion and tenacity were, and are, important to us. My dad, and later my BA and MA at Goldsmiths, and all that I learnt working at Redbus (now Lionsgate UK), the BBC and as a freelance director has led me to think unconventionally, to take risks and put the work in.

My father would never wait passively for success: he pro-actively got out there, networked and pushed doors open for himself. I remember him turning up to see TV execs without an appointment (at the time when you could still turn up unannounced at TV production companies) and ended up fea-turing on three episodes of BBC Two's *Food & Drink,* thanks to his innovative ideas, culinary know-how and personality. One episode saw him and my mum cooking for the Greek Orthodox Archbishop and other priests – something not seen on telly before. He was, and still is, an absolute go-getter, and I seem to take after him!

MY TOP PR TIPS

So, we've established that PR is vital in getting your work seen, but short of sending out your printed blog posts in glass bottles to create attention, how can you make tech work for you? Here's what I've learnt over the years, thanks to Dad and many others who've strengthened my resolve and kept me promoting my work.

Believe in yourself to sell yourself

You've taken the step to set up your own blog, you may have even left full-time employment to make it your career or you're simply going freelance to have more control over your life, work and time. Feel proud of this leap of faith. Now learn to sell yourself.

Get over the fact that someone might say 'no' to you if you try to interview/feature/ask them a question. Most will help as a rule, and 'no' isn't scary anyway. If your request is rejected, don't let it stop you from seeking an alternative. Let it be the catalyst to prove that you can secure someone else. Learning to recover from rejection is the key to success. Chin up, yeah?

Refer back to my confidence tips (see page 72) to remind yourself of your strengths.

Know your USP: your voice and authenticity

Everyone has their own unique selling point (USP), and as a blogger yours is *you* – your voice. You're an original, a one-off, so believe it. Your blog is an imprint of you. Readers often tell me that it's the diversity of my blog they love; that no one day is the same.

It's worth considering what it is that makes your readers keep coming back for more. Is it your style or food posts, or is it sharing the tougher times of family life? Do you help others with allergy-friendly recipes or tips on what to do in London? Harness those qualities and use them to promote yourself to potential readers and journalists. Being dependably yourself elicits trust and coverage.

Don't give up

Despite what you may have learnt from *Ab Fab*, PR isn't all about quaffing champagne and 'Lacroix, sweetie' (if only!). It's actually pretty hard work! PR is an ongoing process and you constantly need to invest time and energy into selling yourself in order to get noticed. I'm not going to lie, publicising yourself can be exhausting, and when you have a backlog of blog posts that need writing, it's easy to push PR aside. Instead, make sure you dedicate a few hours a week to plugging your business. This will help visibility and bring the bucks in. When you secure that sought-after media coverage, don't think you've achieved your goal and can take a break from promotion. Capitalise on this success and use it as a catalyst to find other media opportunities. PR also means featuring on other bloggers' sites and handles. Accept interview requests or initiate them and offer to write guest posts for those you admire.

Media kit/LinkedIn profile

Order business cards, create an online media kit and a LinkedIn profile where you can easily sell yourself and connect with others. Conversation is key, though. Connect in a meaningful way as well as promoting your work. Ask questions and communicate. Share your expertise too.

Say cheese

Good photography can work wonders. Not only does it make your blog feel more professional, but a lot of journalists are more inclined to feature bloggers with their own press shots. Good photography is a worthwhile investment, and clear, well-shot head shots are crucial. Most importantly, always make sure you have hi-res versions of your photos if you are targeting printed media. Create a Pinterest board of portrait shots and practise using your phone. It is worth forking out for a professional photographer: those snaps are part of your personal brand and will help bring in press and paid campaigns.

Make the first move

The world of business often takes me back to dating as a teenager. I used to spend hours building myself up to chat to a boy I liked, truly terrified he might not respond (my eyebrows were much, *much* bigger in those days) but I went for it anyway.

When I first started out as a filmmaker I used to get exactly the same feeling of butterflies, worried that the pitch I had poured my heart and soul into would be rejected. However, I soon realised that this worry would get me nowhere in life, so I did my research, found out the email addresses of the producers I wanted to work with, got in touch, sent them my work and, quite honestly, grew a thick skin. Rejection doesn't bother me anymore. I've learnt that it's all part of the process. One door closes, another opens. Don't let rejection break your confidence or stop you. Dust yourself off and get back out there.

Do you already have any contacts with journalists, researchers in TV, bloggers and vloggers, or do you have friends who can introduce you? Come up with ideas where you can collaborate in a worthwhile way and always think of ways *you* can help others, over how they can help you. You need to come up with ways to create visibility for yourself, starting with your own platforms (where traditional press also looks for inspiration/people to feature/ideas), and you must also proactively reach out on your social media handles to contacts, journalists, TV producers, agents and potential commissioners.

Find out who's who at PR companies you want to work with and contact them, and leave comments on sponsored posts so PRs can discover you. Build up relationships with PRs and those who have worked with you before, and network!

Importantly, approach thought leaders in your field to feature or interview, and collaborate with others. This is the key not only to creative fulfilment and quality content, but also to helping cross-promote one another and reaching new audiences. If I interview a famous singer, for example, and she shares it to her millions of followers on Twitter or Facebook, that offers me exposure to her audience and those who might not already know me.

Offer to write for others for free, in return for PR. Offer original guest posts to reputable, high-ranking sites like BritMums to boost PR and SEO.

Be proactive and seize opportunities – and (like boys) don't wait for them to come to you! The worst they can say is, 'No', and there's plenty more fish (and journalists) in the sea. Next!

Be nice

Sounds obvious, but so many people forget the importance of being personable and kind. The media industry is based on relationships and being nice wins. You might believe yourself to be an island working solo from your kitchen table, but people talk, on- and offline. Be respectful, rise above pettiness and make sure you are always professional online. I know brands that have searched through the entire history of talent on social media to ensure that a person has not behaved in a way that would offend others, or harm the campaign they hope to hire them on.

My publicist friends have informed me that there are certain journalists and bloggers they won't work with as a result of their bad attitude – no matter how good their stats and reach are. Let that be a lesson! They also said that there are certain journalists and bloggers who they will always ensure receive invites to the best events, or get access to exclusive, high-profile interviews, because they have such a good working relationship with them. Remember, if a PR is choosing between you and another blogger who has similar stats, your friendly and professional manner could be the game changer. People pay due diligence so be open, generous with your time and spirit, and exude positive energy and professionalism at all times.

Get social

Make sure you are visible across all the main social media channels, as this is where journalists are most likely to come across your blog. Tweet, Facebook, Pinterest and Instagram handles regularly. Utilise these platforms as much as possible, and make sure you're as professional as possible, creating and sharing quality content. Don't use auto DMs (direct messages) or robots to comment for you anywhere as they are insincere and spammy. Equally, auto-follow and unfollow programs are a no-no.

Use the same, recent photo across all your handles (upload a gravatar – globally recognised avatar – an image that accompanies your email address anywhere online), so your readers know your digital homes. Add your blog link and handles to your email signature too.

Certain platforms work best for your style of content, so see what fits your voice and brand, but target all social media handles to reach the widest audience. Some find Facebook or Instagram work best for their content.

Matt Coyne, viral sensation and bestselling author of *Dummy*, shares his inspirational journey on how Facebook helped him go viral.

'Three months after my son Charlie was born I wrote a post on my personal Facebook page. It was a post on what I'd learned about being a dad so far and it went viral.

Within a week of posting, this thing had been shared hundreds of thousands of times and all over the world ... by bloggers, vloggers, TV, Radio and even movie stars like Ashton Kutcher who described it as "the best description of fatherhood" he'd ever read, which was both ridiculous and very nice of him.

A couple of months after that I set up the Man vs Baby Facebook page and I started to get messages to the page from literary agents asking if I'd thought about writing a book. So, I wrote a couple of chapters, my now agent Euan, took it to the publishers and a week or so later I was signing a book deal. It was an insane and exciting time . . . right up until the point that I realised I had another 70,000 words to write . . . then I shit myself.'

Be contactable

This is perhaps the most basic of rules (but so many people fail at it). You'd be surprised how many blogs I've come across that have no contact details on them at all – or have them buried away as a tiny footer. Make it easy to be discovered. Ensure your contact details are easily accessible to journalists and PRs. These people are extremely busy and don't have time to trawl your blog for an email address.

Make sure your contact page is one click away from your homepage and clearly visible on the header or side menu. Put a contact email form in your blog header that directs to your email, and have all your social buttons visible and at the top of your blog so people can follow and connect with you.

CREATING A BUZZ AROUND THE BIZZ

It's fair to say that I've worked hard at creating a buzz around my blog and getting my work seen. Here are some of the things that have worked for me, and may help you.

Getting a publicist

I did all my own PR until two years ago, when I hired a publicist. Her role quickly morphed into that of a sub-editor, such was the volume of interview and guest post requests that I needed her to upload. She got me some great press and, on reflection, the PR I receive for my personal brand is a diverse mix of social and traditional PR (print and TV), with guest posts and visibility on media platforms. I've since got an in-house book PR at my publishers (to help promote this book you're reading) and a lifestyle PR for my brand.

Plenty of content

Having set up as far back as 2010 helps, as I have since built up a huge archive of material, which helps with SEO (visibility in search engines). Also, producing content consistently (at least once a day, sometimes five times daily) means that I'm found easily by readers and press alike.

Accolades

I also achieved visibility by winning awards and being approached for campaigns early on. It must be noted that I was always proactive in gaining visibility, contacting local and national press about any accolades or interesting films or projects I was working on – and I connected with press and other bloggers from day one. I also posted regularly on the BritMums blog and was featured by other parenting sites, helping to raise my profile.

Emotional connection

The aim is to create shareable content that resonates with others. If you do that, the press will pick it up. As with filmmaking, the key is creating emotion on screen. You want others to connect. Your story is universal – you just need to share it. Plus, once you garner some press, regional as well as national, this inevitably leads to more. As with confidence, the more you achieve, the more you achieve. Online, this is now far easier to do than ever. Traditional press is important but it's tomorrow's chip paper. Online press usually lasts *for ever*. I have blog posts on my site, for example, which I wrote years ago that are still read widely today.

Content that can build

My 'Wonderful Women' interviews, a series started several years ago to champion brilliant women, are some of my most shared posts. These initially originated with me asking over-achieving friends whether I could interview them and share their creative journeys, and quickly evolved to my being offered interviews with famous actors, authors, comedians, bloggers, Olympians and even superstars like Anastacia and Emma Bunton.

Everyone needs PR, and by creating an interview series in a blog, vlog or podcast that's interesting and original, you will create a platform that talent will always want to feature in and that an audience will want to consume. Those pieces or vlogs are then usually shared with the fan base of the contributor – be they a blogger or superstar – allowing you to reach new audiences and acting as PR for you both. Your audience is precious, as is theirs. It works in the same way as content shared by brands. You and your work reaches the brand's fanbase.

As a third tier, the traditional press can also pick up on your piece of activity (stars or not) and feature it in their publication. I also work on campaigns where I'm used 'above the line' (where mass media is used to promote brands and reach out to target consumers), be it radio days, telly or print press. I am regularly pitched to by book PRs too, who enquire whether I want to do an interview piece with their author, or run an original guest post. This is a win-win as my site receives a high-quality piece of work by someone both the public and I admire, and the author receives PR to potential customers for their latest book. These are vital ways to collaborate with creatives – and collaborations are worth their weight in gold online. So, think up ways to host features that will be read and shared, and don't forget to push your own posts.

There are so many ways to promote your work and personal brand. My friend Jessica Huie MBE, publicist and entrepreneur of jhpr.co.uk, highlights its importance:

> 'Endorsement by a third party will always create more impact than you shouting about your brilliance through social media ... What is even more exciting is that the media will delight in showcasing you once you have done the groundwork. Building an online following is your ticket to monetising your creativity and getting featured in the press.'

MANAGEMENT

Having an agent or manager helps with visibility, as he or she has regular meetings with the media/gatekeepers/commissioners to help garner you greater exposure via traditional and digital coverage. Of course, their job is to get you the commissions, handle them and upsell you.

Your manager should share your vision of the brand, ideally helping you brainstorm creatively and, of course, deal with the financial side of the business: negotiating, invoicing and so on. They should also be a good sounding-board who brings out the best in you.

Yes, your manager will usually take between ten and twenty per cent of your entire earnings, but a brilliant one will earn that by elevating your brand and business. Do your research and take the initiative to send out your media kit and blog urls to prospective managers and literary agents.

When it came to this book deal, I was approached by a publishing house after winning a blogging award. This gave me the impetus to seek a literary agent for representation. Whilst scrolling through Instagram, a blogger's profile caught my eye. This led me to her blog and the details of her book and agent. I emailed the agent a short synopsis for my own book idea, with a link to my blog and media kit, and a meeting was set up for the following week. As everything is based on relationships, meeting with agents and managers is critical to establishing whether you'll be able to work with one another. You need to click in-person because you're going to be spending a lot of time together. Your agent and manager must fully believe in you and your potential, as they will be 'selling you' to brands, publishers, press and TV execs. Scan their other clients and the profile of the business to ensure it's a good fit for you.

GET TO KNOW SEO (SEARCH ENGINE OPTIMISATION)

SEO is imperative to the success of your blog. It's the petrol to your car. The beauty of organic SEO is that if you write and share your content regularly and build an archive, an engaged audience will naturally find you. Plus, you are only one post or video away from being a viral sensation – or potentially regarded as someone who is deemed an authority in their field.

Search engines should be your number-one traffic driver if your site is correctly optimised. Offering an answer to a problem or question is what search engines want, and you'll find that your blog and channels can provide insight and support to many.

Mum of two Nic Tuxford is a senior project manager at SEO and digital marketing agency Exposure Ninja (exposureninja. com). Nic's know-how on using SEO to benefit your blog and business meant I had to include her wisdom about how we can all become familiar with SEO.

SEO comprises a number of tools and tactics that website owners can use to improve their ranking positions in search engines such as Google. The better your blog's SEO is, the higher you rank, meaning that the likelihood of people discovering your blog is massively increased. Ever considered why some blogs are at the top of Google and others languish on page nine? The answer, more often than not, is SEO quality. Use SEO correctly and your blog can appear prominently in all kinds of searches relevant to your topic or niche.

Nic explained that in the digital marketing industry, SEO can be used in countless ways to benefit any website. But, when it comes to bloggers, the process can be rather simple: working with high-ranking bloggers provides valuable backlinks and exposure for websites as well-optimised posts. Features such as these create a healthy website – and a healthy website is instantly more desirable to work with. The more SEO-friendly the blog, the better the earning potential for the blogger, too.

Nic advises that the sooner you get your head around SEO, the sooner you'll enjoy the benefits. It will lead to increased traffic for your blog (as search engines should be your biggest driver of traffic), and better PR and sponsorship opportunities.

Whilst SEO can often overwhelm even the most seasoned of bloggers, Nic states that it's vital to question why some blogs rank higher in Google and how you can optimise your own site. Don't view it as a boring tool, despite some duller aspects. Always keep the overall goal in mind . . .

'At its heart, SEO is just about making your blog more appealing: to search engine bots, to readers, and to yourself. Think of SEO like redecorating your house. You want your house to look as awesome as possible, and you have a passion for the overall design that you're going for, so it's important to remember that when you're spending hours on the phone to your electrician.'

Nic pinpoints what you need to do.

Audit your website

Before starting any SEO work, Nic advises you to take an unbiased look at your website, asking an honest friend, family member or fellow blogger to give you a critique of it. Any issues raised can give you an idea of the general aspects that could be turning people away from your blog. For a more technical audit, though, bring in the professionals. Digital marketing agency Exposure Ninja offers a free SEO review.

Here are some of her must-haves for an SEO-friendly website:

- A site that's 'mobile friendly', meaning it can be viewed properly on a phone without squinting!
- Free from broken links
- A quick loading time
- A low bounce rate (the percentage of visitors to a site who navigate away after viewing only one page)

Optimise for strong keywords (but don't over-optimise!)

Nic never stops singing the praises of the WordPress plugin Yoast, so if you self-host a WordPress blog, install it now! The benefit of using the plugin is that it gives you step-by-step targets to properly optimise each blog post for your target keyword.

How do I choose my keywords?

You need to do some strong keyword research. Nic recommends starting with a list of generic long-tailed keywords (a string of words) that are appropriate to your site's niche. These need to be specific and relevant to your ideal reader.

When I asked Nic about how I might rank some of my recipe blogs in Google, the first thing she said to me was: 'Don't try to rank for the term "recipe"!' You see, unless *BBC Good Food*, Jamie Oliver and Allrecipes go out of business, ranking for 'recipe' is going to be tough. So Nic recommended some tools like Keyword Tool. You simply enter your starting point ('recipe') and it produces a selection of long-tailed keywords ('recipe for beef', 'recipe for banana bread', 'recipe for pancakes') that you will have a better chance of ranking for. Here's Nic's thoughts:

'Once you find a keyword you like, you can go one step further and enter it into Moz Keyword Explorer to get the difficulty, opportunity and potential for that keyword. You'll also receive further suggestions for keywords you could target. Bear in mind that you can only search two terms per day with the free account.

With your set of keywords and a clear of idea of which ones to focus on, you now need to know the best way of using them. Create blog content that centres on the topics of the keywords, allowing you to organically use the keywords within the title, subheadings and body text of your blog. 'Organically' is the key here; don't try to cram as many in as possible as this is a strategy that search engines frown upon. As I mentioned at the start, Google is looking to reward and feature content that answers questions and problems, so create blog posts that are useful and clearly solve the issues leading people to punch in these searches.'

Google Trends to the rescue

There are some paid tools that give search volume data (the number of searches for a particular term), but to date no free option has been found to get bulk keyword volumes. The good news is that Google still has some great free tools that are highly useful for SEO for bloggers, outlined below.

Google Trends (trends.google.co.uk) is one of Nic's favourite tools and she feels it is perfect for bloggers:

'If you have a few terms you're considering using in a blog post, you can compare them in Google Trends and it will show you people's interest in them over time. So, let's say you're considering targeting "chicken recipes" and "beef recipes". Type both into Google Trends and you'll see that "chicken recipes" generates far more interest than beef recipes. You shouldn't stop there, though. Go back to your keyword tool and enter "chicken recipes". Now you'll start to hit gold.

The first term that came up for me was "chicken recipes for kids". I can put this into Google Trends and compare it to "beef recipes for kids" and "vegetarian recipes for kids". You'll see that chicken gets the most interest, then vegetarian and then beef. The interest seems to peak at the start of the year. This is probably due to all of those diets people decide to start in January. So, to get the best possible results, jump on the "new year, new me" bandwagon and publish your chicken recipes for kids at the start of the year!

Don't forget to look at the related queries, too. As of January 2017, interest in chicken crockpot recipes is rising by 250%. This is another potential opportunity. But don't forget to research each new term fully. If the competition for a keyword is incredibly high, you'll never reach first page of Google for it.'

Post strong, SEO-friendly content frequently

Google loves fresh, well-optimised content. Nic advises you to aim at posting at least two new blog posts a week. These should be over six hundred words long, optimised for a strong long-tailed keyword (if you're using Yoast, this will be easy).

Nic emphasises the importance of getting these keywords right, as you'll be using them in your blog content, your meta titles and descriptions, and even in your guest posts!

What is the call to action and why should I use one?

As a blogger I love a call to action, as does Nic. A call to action encourages the reader or viewer to act.

Here she offers the following examples of a call to action for a dog-training blog:

- Do you want to hear more about dog training? Sign up to our mailing list
- What are your thoughts on dog training? Any tips I forgot to mention? Comment below!
- Check out my other post about dog training
- Download my FREE dog training guide
- Sign up to my dog training webinar

The aim of the call to action is to keep people on your site, whether that's through offering them something for free or encouraging them to buy something from you. Whatever it takes, give people a reason to stay on your website.

Don't forget internal linking

A simple way to optimise your posts is with internal linking – adding hyperlinks into your blog's text that navigate readers to other pages on your site. Nic points out that it's not only a great way to keep readers on your blog; it can also be great for SEO if you include links to useful, relevant pages.

When you write a new blog post, link back to old posts that are relevant to the new topic, using optimised anchor text (the words you click on to reach the link). Just using 'read more' or 'here' as your anchor text isn't enough for search engines to understand the relevance of your links. Instead, use text that holds value and relevance, like 'get in touch' for a link to your contact details page, or 'dog training webinar' to link to a previous post on that topic.

Create strong meta titles and descriptions

Every blog post and page on your website should have a strong meta title and meta description. Both of these features are alternative, concise pieces of text that appear in search results for your pages, telling users and search engines about the content of the page. These can be created and edited yourself using tools such as the Yoast WordPress plugin (see, we told you it was a great tool!).

Nic points out that there are several good reasons for doing this – and not all of those reasons are directly related to SEO.

The title tag

Your title should contain your target keyword and your description should entice readers to click on your search engine result. Nic likes to think of a meta title as a digital advert for your site. It's good practice to try to get your blog name in there, too:

> 'This isn't just good for SEO. It's good for branding and it helps you to write better. Whether it's a blog post or an entire book, the skill of a great writer is being able to summarise the core idea behind their writing in one sentence or phrase. Title tags force you to do this.'

The description

The Exposure Ninja team are big advocates of getting a unique selling point (USP) into your meta description. So, if you have a giveaway on your blog, Nic advised getting the word *'win'* as close to the start of your description as is natural in order to make the description stand out.

If you are using Yoast to enter your title tag and description, you'll get a warning if the description is too short or long. However, Exposure Ninja's rule of thumb is around 65 characters for a title tag and 155 characters for a description.

Offsite SEO for bloggers

Nic said that one of her biggest pet hates is seeing SEO guides advising bloggers to spam comment as a means to improving SEO. She said: 'By all means, comment on a blog post you enjoyed reading and link to your own site, but please don't waste valuable time commenting on fifty-odd blogs a day if it isn't meaningful and on relevant, influential blogs.'

At Exposure Ninja, they value three sources of backlinks:

- High-authority directories

- Video-sharing websites
- Guest posts on websites/blogs with a similar niche

As a blogger, you're unlikely to have a business address, so your directory-listing opportunities may be limited. Still, you should ensure you get a brand page on Google My Business, a Facebook page and are included in directories for bloggers.

If you enjoy vlogging, Nic suggests starting a YouTube account if you haven't already. Don't forget other sharing sites either, such as Dailymotion, Wistia and Flickr, which all provide opportunities to share videos. Each can come equipped with a backlink to your website in the account description and in the video description.

Finally, Nic says, the most valuable link opportunities come via guest posting:

'You can start small, posting on a fellow blogger's site, and eventually try pitching ideas to larger publications and online magazines. I would recommend aiming to write at least one guest blog post per month to increase your organic backlink profile.'

What about social media?

It's still not clear whether there is a link between social shares and SEO for bloggers. Google says not, but studies have shown correlations between highly shared online content and search engine rankings. Given that social shares will inevitably increase traffic to your site, Nic confirms that it's certainly a good idea to embrace social media.

For more in-depth information on digital marketing, read Exposure Ninja's book *How to Get to the Top of Google*.

MY FAVOURITE SOCIAL MEDIA HANDLES

Facebook

A popular handle, particularly for the over thirties, it's a slow grower – like its sister handle Instagram – as the algorithm favours paid boosts. However, it's a vital platform to feature on and interact with your followers. I share between three to five times a day, sharing one blog post of my own, and three or more general, (mostly) humorous shares from other pages that resonate. I love to upload video content natively there, and these pieces tend to receive more views for me than on YouTube, a place my audience seems to only recently be embracing.

Instagram

This is a visual handle where you can connect with a like-minded audience. I usually keep to bold colours in my gallery (mostly red) and share video and photos mostly around fashion and lifestyle. Don't forget hashtags too. I like to use these on my fashion photos:

> #personalstyle #mumstyle #latergram #outfitideas #fashiondaily #fashionmum #fashionstylist #fashionable30s #outfitshare #streetstyle #stylish30s #styleoftheday #Lwiw #wiwt #whatiwore #ootd #myoutfit #outfitinspiration #outfitpost #spotmystyle #iworethis #styleblogger #instastyle #styleover30 #mumboss #instalook #fbloggers #nailedit

Twitter

This is a handle that enables you to connect with followers, readers, esteemed authors, celebrities and members of the press. It's the literary lovers' favourite handle and the use of hashtags and trending topics allows you to achieve greater visibility for your own work or point of view in real time. I schedule tweets mostly focusing on evergreen content such as parenting and food. I also enjoy taking part in, and hosting, relevant Twitter parties for brands, which encourages discussion around themes and products.

Twitter started as a handle that broke news and it continues to do so.

Pinterest

Pinterest, despite being public, feels like my own curated online space where I collate boards based on my interests. You can also create private boards for your own reference. There are two kinds of images on Pinterest: editorial images that tend to be incredibly beautiful, and infographic-style images or those with titles encouraging you to click to blogs. I include a mix when it comes to my content, but mostly share editorial-style images.

Content builds profile, so look at what you can create yourself: posts, social posts, videos, newsletters, podcasts and lives. Consistently sharing quality content with integrity is the key.

Chapter 8

HAPPILY EVER AFTER?

The truth is, life never remains stagnant. It's always in flux, and that's the beauty of it. None of us can predict what's coming next – a bit like the ever-evolving tech world. You'll face challenges day to day, maybe even minute to minute – we all do, and no more so than as a working mum looking after little people, while meeting tight deadlines. I promise you this, however: with dedication, patience and as much support as you can muster, you *will survive* and *thrive* at both work and home.

If I can, you can. In this chapter, I wrap up how.

If you want something enough, and you're prepared to work for it, you will overcome the times you feel like quitting, and you will endure. But, having read this book, you know that already, right? You now have the tools and strength to look challenges in the eye, confident you can overcome them, certain you have the right to feel *fired* up and excited about the future. That it's in your hands, literally. All you need is a laptop, a domain name and some ideas. It's time, mamas (and papas)!

I hope your biggest takeaway from this book has been the

knowledge that once you discover what you love (by trying lots of different things and not just necessarily following one path), you find renewed vigour and feel excited about working again after kids. My hope is that you will jump out of bed looking forward to writing your heart out, creating content you can share instantly, developing a brand that means the world to you – or, if you decide to head back to work, you feel confident in your ability and potential to contribute.

When you feed your soul, everything else will follow. Work hard first and trust that recognition will come – especially in this democratic digital world where the brave and the doers are endlessly renumerated. It won't all be all chocolate brownies, unicorns and rainbows, of course. How vanilla would that be? The juggle is real and 'hello hormones', so be prepared to veer between feeling like a sassy queen one day and doubting yourself with a mega-dose of mama guilt the next. Accept this rollercoaster for what it is, a ride, but know the pain gets easier and the rewards are worth it in the end.

I crack on through all the shizz I need to wade through, even when I feel I'm failing, and so should you. Return to page 56 and my reinvigorating self-care tips if you feel you're forgetting yourself and need a boost. Mum (and Dad) comes first OK? Without your strength, everyone suffers.

Yes, you will ache for those kids of yours when you're apart, but you will soon find your groove, and the pros will outweigh the cons before you know it. It's back to finding balance.

If I don't have structured time and fun with my kids – be it homework or swimming lessons – and miss out on precious time with them, I feel I'm lacking in my role as a parent, and I can't bring my A game to my job either. If I'm not happy at work, it affects my mood at home. I need to do both as best I can for harmony to exist in each corresponding world. I've not got this balance nailed, by the way. I've just learnt that it's OK to feel overwhelmed and that I'm dropping balls at times, because I will. You will too.

Dropping the kid off in his uniform on non-uniform day, or mixing up the dates for parent's evening, are just two of my f**k-ups, but nobody died – I managed to get my child back home and changed before the bell rang, and the teacher squeezed me into a late appointment when I appealed to her at the school gates. There isn't always a happy ending, like the time I got the Nativity dates wrong, missed my kid in it and sobbed for hours (me not him).

Experience tells me that I've always managed to overcome the crap times. I've endured (cried when I felt like it), and I shall continue to. That's the silver lining to adversity, I suppose. However big or small the problem, it teaches you how capable you are. What you are made of. That doesn't mean you mustn't shout out for help when you need it. Every #mumboss knows it takes a (virtual and ideally, real) village to raise a family, and it takes a community to raise a mumboss so she can reach her potential.

The mumboss mindset is all about treating yourself as you would your best friend – with love and respect. Guilt needs to be shown the door or quietened at the very least. Stop feeling bad about wanting to do a job you love. My kids inspired my career change. They've made me who I am today, and I'm proud of that fact. Without them I wouldn't be a boss. Plus, however hard it might seem to carve out time for a passion project as a busy mum, remember that millions of women are doing just that. Some are juggling multitudes of jobs and still coming home to write, sell clothes on eBay or blog at 1am. Think of the strongest women you know and know that that same strength exists in you too if you fancy trying something new.

Take this book that I've written by candlelight (OK, not *actual* candlelight, but my bedside light), while everyone else slept around me. I got into the flow of writing *Mumboss* at night once my blog work and parental duties were done, sacrificing sleep because I wanted to write it. Forget 'wanted'. *I had to write this book.* Not because I signed a contract – although, yes, that too – but because this book was *bigger* than me. It had a life of its own. It wrote itself. I was just the vehicle for committing it to paper.

I had to share my experience, because I owed it to my readers, myself and my kids to make sense of my life and job, in order to help others by sharing what I know. I also needed to show my kids that when you commit to something, you get the job done. They watched me furiously bang away at my laptop, returning to it at all hours with a dedication to deliver. They've watched me work for a year on something that meant the world to me.

I needed to lead by example and show them that we must work hard in order to achieve; that however hard life gets, we don't quit. And that projects of the heart require stamina and strength. I lost my young auntie Zak before submitting the final draft of this book, and despite very little sleep, a broken heart and eyes I could barely open due to my overwhelming grief, I found the strength somehow to finish the book in your hands. I felt hollow from sorrow, but I let the words flow, I committed to my craft and gave this book my very best shot. That's all I ask of you when you commit to working too. To have a go, to make some sacrifices, to put yourself first for the good of everyone else. Every word and day back at work will be worth it, as it is for me. Why? Because I want to make a difference to those who read this book and to succeed in creating what I've set out to deliver.

Mumboss, the book, mattered to me, as do you, kick-ass reader, so I made the time (despite not having much of it) to put the work in, to show up and deliver. I grafted and I grafted hard. I always do and that's 'the not-so-secret' secret of my success. I also put my trust in the ebb and flow of my mumboss life, while keeping my eye on the big picture at all times: that I one day hope to follow in the footsteps of Oprah and Shonda Rhimes. I know, *big aspirations baby*! We mustn't lose our ability to dream our dreams though, right?

I know the rhythm of my work/life now: intense periods of work, followed by a brief chance to breathe and rest as new deals are made, deliverables confirmed, more work sprints and endless juggling commence once again. The cycle goes like this: new projects, deadlines, growth and rest. Like waves, work comes in and out intensity-wise, and my priority is to ride those waves and to reach out for a life jacket when I feel I'm drowning. Having that emotional first-aid kit to hand, which you all know about now (meditation, yoga, time out and a therapist if things feel too much) is what empowers me. I now know that help is there if I need it.

Experience has taught me what I need to succeed as a working parent: the ability to negotiate, delegate and organise well, and a bit of distraction for good measure. The struggle exists, but like childbirth, it's worth it for the *love* of it. A passionless life is not worth living.

The fulfilment my job gives me – the act of producing work time and time again in a way that connects and resonates with others, or that sparks a debate or even changes my own mind – is what *keeps me going*. I started my blog identity-less and lost, and now, rather like procreating, I have a living, breathing technical baby in my blog, which feeds me, creatively, and my family, literally.

WHY IT'S WORTH IT

Below I share some pros of my working life to remind you that the good fight is worth it.

Work makes me a better mother

I get to enjoy the sweet pleasure of doing something that nourishes me every day, in a job that never feels like work, despite the sweat, tears and hours of labour. By carving out a job I love, I'm able to be a kinder, more patient mother to my kids.

Author and actress Sara Alexander (evaalexander.com), who has appeared in *Harry Potter and the Deathly Hallows*, *Doctor Who* and Franco Zeffirelli's *Sparrow*, shares my view:

'I escaped into my writing. I snatched time while the toddlers slept. Not every day at first, but over time, like them, the practice became woven deep into the fabric of our lives. In our household, we developed code "yellow mask". Like on planes, reminding one another to attend to ourselves before saving those around you.

My creative life is the only place I can fortify myself for the twists and turns of motherhood. It's the place I can swim in the unknown, uncharted waters of a chapter, choppy and changeable. Writing, like parenting, requires real life to hone it and a great deal of endurance.'

Flexibility

I get to see my children more than any other job I've had before. It's flexible and also actively involves my kids as I document our lives.

Love

The love, sense of community and close friendships I've made thanks to my digital life make up for trolls any day of the week.

No regrets

I want to live without regrets. I won't buckle and walk away when my creative life feels hard-going. I will prevail, safe in the knowledge all will work out in the end. It sounds hippy-dippy, but I trust the universe and the timing of my life and so should you.

Legacy

Witnessing my parents' pride, in particular, warms my heart. My dad likes to remind me that I'm making my mark as a British-Greek Cypriot woman, and that legacy means a lot to me.

I'm sure you can add many more of your own. Make your own list and put it in your purse so that when you feel rejected and dejected (as we all do at times), or are simply overtired, you have a magical list to help remind you of your purpose, getting you back on track.

THE TRAPS OF SUCCESS

Once you're on your way, there is of course the danger of social media obsession, of living online more than off. I take regular digital detoxes, even if it's just for a few days, especially on holiday, and I try to keep off my phone on weekends and at night (when I'm not writing a book), so I get to spend quality time with those I love and simply be in the moment.

Yes, you are passionate about your business, but don't forget to *live*. Equally, while it's wonderful to be celebrated, *don't believe the hype*. Keep your feet on the ground, your real friends close and your 'rider list' in your head. Don't be a ding-bat!

AND REMEMBER – DON'T GET
BOGGED DOWN BY NUMBERS

Mumbosses know that quality content is what matters first and foremost. Create the work and the stats will come. Maybe you've recently set up an online business, but have become so caught up in growth that you've forgotten to focus on substance. Stop, collaborate and listen – Vanilla Ice style.

There are no shortcuts, not long term anyway, and nobody wants to be a flash-in-the-pan creator. We are here to stay, to make our mark on the world, mumbosses, to share our story so others feel they can too.

It's human nature to want approval, to seek it and relish it – both online and in real life – but we must look to those who know us, for their honesty and, equally, we must self-reflect and self-validate so our own moral compasses can be fine-tuned and not clouded by flattery and fame, however big or small . . . Admittedly, I can treat myself like shit too, of course, and be my own worst critic, but that's where my support network comes in. The people in it help me see the wood for the trees. They tell me when I'm being a dick, and when I'm not and need to high-five myself. I'm the first to throw my hands up when I'm in the wrong and apologise. I've learnt to kill pride and do the right thing.

While it's important to keep an eye on growth and engagement if blogging and vlogging is your business, don't let it consume, or define you. On the other hand, don't feel you have to follow the crowd. Being you is your strength. Just 'do you'!

It's easy to become trapped in a herd-like mentality – to believe others are better, smarter and more creative than you because they have 2789405664 times more followers than you do, but that's not how *art* works. Art is subjective. 'Since the start of time' subjective, by the way. And we are all artists, whether we're tweeting short stories of our lives, making animation films or painting with brushes. It's a need, a desire, a therapy and life-long love. As Seth Godin says:

> 'If it weren't for the ups and downs, we could just stay at home and keep our work in the attic. We put it into the world pre-cisely because of the challenge.'

Our desire is to express and share, however many people con-sume it. The act itself of sharing something publicly is exciting and nourishing, and was, pre-internet, only for the minority. So, next time you ponder why you don't have one thousand retweets on that hilarious tweet of yours, or one hundred comments on your Facebook page, remember what actually matters and go back to your art. Your work. What feeds you. How writing makes you feel. Don't let that desire to be liked prevent you from creating the work you like yourself. Channel that anxious, needy energy into doing what makes you happy.

I find positivity in social media, for the most part, and my driving force is being able to write posts and make videos. Everything else is secondary. I want people to read and watch my work, but I'd do it regardless.

The question 'Why?', in terms of finding purpose, has come up a lot and *Marie Claire*'s deputy editor Andrea Thompson reminds us of this when doubt hits:

> 'Ask yourself "Why"? WHY are you doing this business? Why is it important to you? Why does it matter? Why does it make you happy? So many people get caught up in running a business they forget to really examine their motivations. Ask yourself "Why?" It helps you focus and keeps you focused on your goals when things get tough.'

You don't need to know it all or to have an action plan in place before you hit publish. I often don't know how my career will evolve from week to week. You just need the will to begin and keep going.

As my hero Maya Angelou so wisely said, 'A bird doesn't sing because it has an answer. It sings because it has a song' and the song is within us all. It's time to focus on getting your song out there, building your creative business or getting back to work and making your dreams come true. In being who you want to be.

To all my strong, smart and sassy creative mumbosses, please don't underestimate yourselves, sit up and seize the opportunity to share your voice – the world (wide web) is waiting!

ACKNOWLEDGEMENTS

This is going to read like a transcribed Oscar speech, but there really are so many people to thank for the birth of my third baby: *Mumboss*. It's taken a city, never mind a village, to raise this mumboss, and it truly requires a perfect storm to write a book!

Firstly, I must thank my very own #mumboss mother, Vasoulla, who quit her PhD when I was nine months old because she couldn't bear to be apart from me, transitioning from lecturing at universities to becoming a successful restaurateur with my dad, George, showing me what the #mumboss way of life looked like from the age of two. My mum found a flexible way to work and raise her family back then in the 1980s, and is the smartest and most selfless person I know. She endlessly inspires me with how honest, fair and loving she is, and I'm grateful to have her as my blueprint. Thank you mama.

Thank you, too, to my dad, 'Papa G', who along with my mum has always championed me. He has encouraged my film-making endeavours since childhood, and instilled in me that anything I set my mind to is possible (however crazy). He has also never stopped banging on at me about getting Greek Cypriots on the map, so I hope this book helps his cause a tiny, little bit!

Thanks too to my brother, Solos, for all the fun times and

being the 'Wogan' to my 'Kylie' as we made home videos as kids. Those were just the start of it all . . .

Endless love and respect to my husband Peter, my grounding rock and the love of my life. Thank you always for your wisdom, care and calm demeanour – and of course thank you to my wonderful children, Oliver and Alexander, for making me a mumboss and showing me the meaning of unconditional love. Their excitement for my job knows no bounds and all I've heard this year has been 'Mummy, you're going to have a book in the library!'

Thank you too to Robyn Drury, my original agent, who, despite moving on to become an editor early on in this process, was a catalyst to all that came after and whose passion and insight had a huge impact on this book. Thanks also to my current agent, Diane Banks, for her sharp eye and infinite encouragement.

Huge thanks to Jillian Young, my brilliant editor, for her passion for *Mumboss* and belief in me; for her clarity, judgement and friendship, and for making this process one I'll never forget. Thank you too to Anna Steadman, who took over as editor when Jillian went on maternity leave. Anna understood my vision from the get-go and her reassuring chats and input always got the best out of me. Thanks also to Jillian Stewart for her on-going editorial support.

My thanks also to Neil Ransome for his encouragement while I wrote this book.

Special thanks to my great friend, hair stylist Jason Collier, who keeps my hair looking fabulous and who got the wind machine in all the right places for the book cover (!). Thanks to Joseph Sinclair who takes the best photos ever and make-up artist Lauren Kay for making me wish I woke up looking like I do on the book cover, every single day!

So much love and gratitude to every single contributor in this book (I adore you all – told you it was an Oscar speech) and all my love to my closest and oldest mates Carlie Berger and Caroline Asquith, who have taken it in turns to hold my hand, laugh until we cried, and supported me through some of the hardest times of my life.

Huge thanks too to all of my tribe, my wonderful friends: Uju Asika, Mirka Moore, Lela London, Sharmin de Vries, Ursula Tavender, Libby Cussen, Rachael Dennis, Nicci Topping, Jacqui Paterson, Nomita Vaish Taylor, Zaz Grumbar, Juliet McGratton, Michelle Reeves, Maggy Woodley, Joana Mateus, Hayley Johnson, Julie Green, Lucy Hird and William Wynn-Jones.

I'm also forever indebted to my close friend Amancay Tapia, who encouraged me to start a blog in the first place! Thank you for pestering me, I owe you so much!

Lots of love and thanks also to my mentor and good friend Harriet Thorpe, who is always there for me, and to Jessica Huie MBE and Natasha Courtenay-Smith for their endless support and encouragement. Thank you too to my designer Amee D'Souza for her super work on my blog.

Empowered women empower women.

Deepest thanks, too, to psychologist Toby Chelms, who helped put me back together again Humpty-Dumpty style after my traumatic birth and thereafter. I will always be grateful to him for helping me to help myself.

I also owe so much of my success in both work and life to my formative years studying at Goldsmiths, University of London, and to my lecturer and friend John Beecham who is sadly no longer with us but whose work continues to impact my career, daily. Goldsmiths gave me the guts and know-how to think outside the box and always search for ways to break new ground in meaningful ways.

Thank you to my beloved auntie Zak who got to see this book's cover before she passed away and who was incredibly proud of all that I have achieved. Zak has inspired me to be a better human being, to rise above pettiness, always forgive, and to do the right thing. I know she's always by my side.

Thank you too to all of my Big Fat Greek family for their love and support, it means so much.

Last, but by no means least, thank you, thank you, thank you to my readers, followers and digital friends who get me out of bed each and every morning: I have a blog, and now a book, because of you guys. This book is for you. I hope it inspires a mass of mumbosses in its wake and helps us all continue to thrive both at work and at home.

Please tag my book with #mumboss and #mumbossbook, start your blogs and businesses today, or return to work with confidence, and please don't doubt yourselves, you hear. Crack on!

Vicki x

INDEX

A

'above the line' stars 189, 190
Absolutely Fabulous 75, 181
acceptance 131
accolades 187–8
action plans 62, 210
Adams, John 50
Additional Maternity Leave 29
Adele 42
advertising i, 9, 31, 154
Advertising Internet Bureau i
affirmation 57, 58
Africa 13
Alexander (son) 25, 29, 68, 212
     birth of 11, 42, 52, 53
     separation from 140–1
Alexander, Sara 206
All Baby Advice
     (allbabyadvice-blog.com) 110
Allrecipes 193
Anastacia 12, 188
Angelou, Maya 10, 210
anxiety 41, 44, 75–6, 140, 141
The Apprentice 126
The Art of Dramatic Writing (Egri)
     125
art(s) 7, 77, 85, 89, 109–10, 134–5
     healing nature of 128
Asika, Uju 10, 63, 213
Asquith, Caroline 38–9

assertiveness 102
Atwood, Margaret 162
Australia 13, 78
authenticity 74, 160, 181
avatars 185
awards i, 10, 17
awesomeness, recognising 85

B

Babes About Town
     (babesabouttown.com) 10,
     63
babies:
     boring bits 23, 23n
     and first-time motherhood 8
     first words 23n
     as schedulers 8, 9
     sleep patterns of 37, 45
baby blues 43–50
baby book 57–8
Baby Jake 21
balance 14, 63, 66, 112, 123, 136,
     137–8, 144, 163, 203
BBC 10, 16, 21, 147, 180, 193
Beckham, Victoria 35
Becoming a Writer (Brande) 132
belief, in oneself 180–1
Berger, James 9
Beyoncé 102
Bieber, Justin 23

birth:
    benefits of 139–40, 205
    celebrating experience of 55
    how-to video 44
    and mental health 42
    mother's mental health after 52
    nesting mode 57
    partners support during 50–2
    plans 26
    practicalities of 40–3
    second time around 52–3, 113
    trauma 41–2, 45, 50–2
blessings, counting 130
blog(s)/blogging 18, 117 (*see also*
    vlogging)
    'above the line' 189, 190
    archive material 187
    audience, *see* demographics
    audit 192–3
    being pushy 163
    bonus content 172
    children's fashion 120
    competitions 170, 172
    content, choosing 155–6, 160–1
    creating buzz around 187
    DIY 120
    filming for 137
    first movement 74
    food 118–20
    highs and lows 13, 14
    honest 21
    how to approach 108–10
    identity 205
    interiors 120
    internal linking 196–7
    investors 172
    joy of 127
    keys to success 70, 71, 72–81
    linking ('linkys') 171
    monetising 9
    niche 12, 162
    'parties' 171
    photographs 182
    platform, choosing 157–8
    posting regime 163

    PR, *see main entry*
    ranking 165, 166
    routine after 164
    self-hosting 167, 193
    stability offered by 142
    starting small 67–9
    traffic 155, 164
    true gift of 10
    two-way-street nature of 159
    as vehicle for confidence 72
    Vicki sets up 7–8, 10, 74–5, 77
    viral content 185–6
    what to write 107–10
    when to 132
    YouTube-channel 142
blue light, and sleep patterns 56
Blue Peter 41
body consciousness 35–6
Bonnell, Laura 113–14
Bradford College 9
Brady, Karen 68
brainstorming 80, 190
brand essence 97
Brande, Dorothea 132
branding 11, 14, 80, 108, 117, 128,
    130, 153, 155, 157, 161, 167
    personal, how to create 158–60
    psychologist 159
Branson, Richard 124
'brave face' syndrome 25, 44–5,
    47
breastfeeding 12, 44, 52, 66, 140
Brennan, Kay 38
Brilliance in Blogging Awards 10
#Brilliantblogposts 171
British Gas 9
British Library v, 13, 146
BritMums 10, 184, 187–8
BritMums Brilliance in Blogging
    Awards v
Brittas Empire 75
Broadbent, Vicki:
    awards v, 10
    blog created by 7–8, 10, 18
    charitable work 7, 12

childhood 15–19
children, *see* Alexander; Oliver
creativity of 6–7, 14, 17, 18, 61, 161–2
as digital ambassador 11
early work experience of 126
education 5–6, 7, 16, 160, 179–80, 213
Facebook page of 164
filmmaking career of v, 3, 6, 6–7, 10, 10–11, 14, 16, 16–17, 76–7, 101, 137, 142, 143, 154, 165, 180
first pregnancy 32
first-time motherhood 7, 17, 17–18, 23
'guru' of 10
husband, *see* Peter
maternal instinct 24, 27
online diary of 15
online supporters of 124
'Pied Piper' sobriquet 5
teaching career of 5–6
transformation of 77
workshop co-hosted by v, 13
writing career of v, 3, 6–7, 9, 206, 216
'zero to hero' 153
Broken 17
bullying 121–30
Bunton, Emma 12, 188
business, setting up, top tips 92–4
business cards 114, 170, 183, 185
business-mindedness 1
business planning:
    accounts 173–8
    and promotion 178–9
    top tips 92–4
buzz, how to create 187

C
caesarean section (C-section) 17, 34, 38–9, 41, 45–6, 53–5, 159
    elective 42, 53–5
camaraderie 88, 141, 159
Cameron-Kitchen, Tim 166

candidness 49, 95, 138
career coaching 159
Carlie (best friend) 35
CBeebies 21
CBT (cognitive behavioural therapy) 48, 49
celebrity 117, 154, 186, 188, 200, 205, 208, 212
Channel 4 v, 17
charitable work 57
Chelms, Toby 47, 48, 50, 75, 213
childcare 30, 65, 66, 93, 106, 121, 146, 149–50
children:
    parents influenced by 9
    as schedulers 9
chilling out 92, 145, 150
Citizens Advice 65
Clance, Pauline 99
Clark, Laura 52
co-parenting 136, 144–5, 150
Cochrane, Nikki 64
cognitive behavioural therapy (CBT) 48, 49
collaboration 77–81, 126
comfort zone 60, 132
communication, importance of 29
comparison 81–3
comparison paralysis 84–6
compassion 139
Competition Database (competitiondatabase.co.uk) 171
compromise 13, 110, 137, 139, 141, 150
confidence 3, 63, 70, 71, 183
    -boosters 94–6
    how to build 59, 59–60
    regaining 67
    in work 87–90
confidence conundrum 31–40
confidence-fail 59
contactability 186
context 84
counselling 48, 49

Courtenay-Smith, Natasha 72–3,
116–18, 153, 213
Coyne, Charlie 186
Coyne, Matt 22, 185–6
creativity 7–8, 26, 82, 106, 111–12,
132–5, 161, 189
boosters 132–5
joy of 127
surrounding yourself with
135
Creator Academy 73
criticism:
constructive, benefit of 128
how to handle 95, 126–30
cross-promotion 110, 184

D
Dad Blog UK (dadbloguk.com) 50
The Dad Network (thedadnetwork.
co.uk) 33
dadboss 3
dairy products 118–19
magnesium in 52
date nights 57, 151
Day Lewis, Daniel 69–70
deadlines 110, 144, 205
meeting 137, 139, 148–9, 168,
201
demographics 161–2, 169, 188, 200
dependability 168
depression 42–50 (*see also specific
conditions*)
Dhokia, Raj 173–7 *passim*
diary keeping 57–8, 91
dedication 12, 73, 101, 133, 145,
154, 164, 182, 201, 204
diet 34, 52, 118–19, 162
digital advert 197
digital detox 130
Digital Mums (digitalmums.com)
64
digital-storytelling 3
direct messaging (DM-ing) 185
Disney-effect 6
distraction 131–2

Dixon, Alesha 12
to-do lists 67, 138
Do Something Different Ltd 91–2
Doctor Who 206
'doing me' 74
domain authority (DA) 166–7
downtime 93
Dragon's Den 147
drama, avoiding 129
Dream It, Do It, Love It (Griffiths) 111
drjulietmcgrattan.com 34
*Dummy: The Comedy and Chaos of
Real-Life Parenting* (Coyne) 22,
185

E
eBay 203
education:
after becoming a parent 144
Vicki's 5–6, 7, 16, 160, 180, 213
Egri, Lajos 125
emotional connection 188
employment *see* work
empowerment 53, 96–8
endorphins 37, 49, 56
equilibrium 139
e-shops 120, 154
Etsy 28, 31, 65
exercise 34, 37–9, 56, 107, 110, 148,
205
exhaustion 47, 92
experience, importance of 165–6
Exposure Ninja (exposureninja.
com) 164, 166, 191, 197, 198

F
Facebook 62, 77, 81, 100, 155, 157,
158, 164, 169, 170, 184, 185, 186,
199–200
groups 171
Honest Mum page 164
Like and Share competitions
171
Man vs Baby page 186
pages 160, 170, 186, 198, 210

Facebook Live 157
Facebook Lives 11
faking it 69
fatherhood, describing 186 (*see also*
    parenthood)
fatigue 23, 35
fear, combating 68, 75–7, 98
feelings 41, 83, 95–6, 100, 128, 159
Ferguson, Al 33
finances, how to handle 173–8, 190
financial security 4, 10, 27, 83, 93,
    100, 106, 115, 138, 149
Fine, Phanella Mayall 126, 127
first-time parenthood, *see*
    fatherhood; motherhood;
    parenthood
fitness, *see* exercise 107
Fitness 4 Mamas (fitness4mamas.
    com) 110
flexibility 206
Food & Drink 16, 180
4Talent v
free-fall 133
Free From Fairy (freefromfairy.
    com) 118
Friends 22
friendship 125–6
Frozen 45
Future Shapers Live v

G
game-changers 46, 151, 185
Ghostwritermummy.co.uk 49
gig-economy 174
goal-setting 1, 117
Godin, Seth 152, 209
Goldsmiths, University of London
    16, 160, 180, 213
Good Food 193
good intentions 148
Good Morning Britain 11
Good to Know v, 11
Google 14, 73, 161, 163, 167, 191,
    192, 194–5
    crawl budget 164

Google Analytics 76, 138, 161, 169
Google Trends 194–5
Google+ 185, 199
grammar and punctuation 108
Grammarly 72
gratitude diary 57
gravatars 185
Grazia Daily v, 12
Grenglish (grenglish.co.uk) 32
Griffiths, Lucy 111–12
Groundhog Day 23
Grumbar, Zaz 115, 213
guilt 99, 136–51 (*see also* impostor
    syndrome)
overcoming 91, 140–2

H
Harry Potter 42, 206
hashtags v, 1, 3, 36, 169, 171, 203,
    211, 214
importance of 200
Headspace 49
health, *see* exercise
healthy eating 118–19
herd-like mentality, avoiding 208
Hesz, Sarah 78, 172
Hirlam, Stacey 143–4
HMRC 174–7 *passim*
'honest mum', definition of 123
Honest Mum (honestmum.com) v,
    1, 4, 10, 15, 18, 30, 80, 111, 164,
    166, 177
    Facebook page 164
    as limited company 174
    'Wonderful Women' series 12,
        188
    Work With Me page 74, 168
Honestmum Limited 174
honesty 96
hormonal dysfunction 140
How to be a DIVA at Public Speaking
    (Kaye) 76
Huffington Post v, 12, 164
hugging, healing properties of 57
Huie, Jessica v, 13, 67, 189, 213

hustling 87, 105–6, 112, 134, 160

I
ICP (intrahepatic cholestasis of
     pregnancy) 24, 34, 41
Imes, Suzanne 99
impactful content 168
impostor syndrome 81, 99–104 (*see
     also* guilt)
independence 115, 149
inequality, in the workplace 4
infertility 27
influencers 74, 106, 153–4
inner critic, how to silence 94
innovation 95, 156, 180
insights 169
Instagram 81, 105, 155, 157, 158,
     164, 169, 170, 185, 190, 199, 200
integrity 3, 19, 85, 122, 201
internal dialogue, how to control
     102
internal linking 196–7
internet:
     embracing 128
     as level playing field 15
     traffic 155, 164
intrahepatic cholestasis of
     pregnancy (ICP) 24, 34, 41
investors 172
IPSE 65
IVF 27, 32

J
Jackson, Michael 22, 53
jhpr.co.uk 189
job-sharing 29
joie de vivre 6
journal writing 15
#journorequest 169
juggling 134, 136–51, 202, 203, 205

K
Kaye, Shola 76
keywords 193–4
'kind to yourself' list 39

kindness 129
Kona Seven (konaseven.uk) 173
Kutcher, Ashton 186

L
Labour Party 70
Langton, Penny 63
laughter, healing properties of 57
Le Coin De Mel (lecoindemel.com)
     65
leadership 3, 70, 96, 109
     muscle memory 68–9
Leadersmithing (Poole) 68
Lean In (Sandberg) 100
lecnutrition.co.uk 52
Letterman Co. 113
legacy 98, 207
leverage 152
Lewis, Anna 30–1
liability 174–5
life coaching 29
limited companies 173–4
Linchpin (Godin) 152
LinkedIn 164, 172, 182
linking ('linkys'), online 171
Lionsgate UK 180
Little Britain 54
'looking fine', how to perfect 47
Loquax (loquax.co.uk) 171
loss 113–14
love 208

M
McBride, Hillary 124
McDonagh, Margaret 70
McDonalds 162
McGrattan, Juliet 34, 43, 107, 213
Macguire, Sharon 12
McRobbie, Linda Rodriguez 8
Madonna 15
magnesium 52
mailing lists 171–2
Man vs Baby 186
management 189–91
Marie Claire v, 12, 209

maryonstewart.com 139
mass media 185
Massie-Taylor, Katie 78, 172
maternal instinct 24, 26
maternity leave 28–31, 33, 64, 106
Matthews, Cerys 12
Mayfair gallery 7
'me' time 3, 57, 145–51
meanness 121–30
media kits 168, 182, 190
Mel (friend) 65–6
melatonin 55
mental health 42, 48–50, 52, 139
    (see also depression; specific
    conditions)
meta descriptions 197–8
meta titles 197
MichelleReevesCoaching.com 29
The Million Dollar Blog
    (Courtenay-Smith) 72, 116, 153
mingling 170
Minogue, Kylie 15, 212
Mirka (friend) 110
moderation 137
Mohr, Tara 62, 89, 109–10
Montague, Vicki 118–20
moo.com 170
Morgan, Piers 11
Mother Nature 26
motherhood (see also parenthood):
    demystifying 25
    irony of 111
    and maternity leave, see main
        entry
    preparing for 20–6
    and work 26–31, 143
motivation 13, 62, 77, 82, 93, 94,
    116, 131, 142, 146, 209
movie watching 57
moving on 52–5, 102–3, 212
Moz (moz.com/researchtools/ose/)
    167, 194
Muggle mums 42
multitasking 26
'mum guilt' 99 (see also guilt;

impostor syndrome)
'mum tums' 35
Mumbelievable (www.
    mumbelievable.com) 57, 146
mumboss:
    definition of 1, 4
    equations 61–2, 70, 83
    hook-ups 78
    pearls of wisdom 3
    trademark 177
#mumboss 1, 200, 203, 211, 214
muscle memory 68
Mush (letsmush.com) 172
music 22, 53, 102, 133–4
    benefits of 57

N
Nappy Valley 114
natashacourtenaysmith.com 72,
    116
National Institute of Mental Health
    (NIMH) 47, 48
naysaying 13, 62, 80, 105, 121–30
NCT classes 45
negativity 102, 105, 121–30
    avoiding 56
nesting mode 57
Netflix 145, 151
networking 71, 169–72
'new life', how to achieve 142–3
newsletters 170, 171, 201
NHS 46, 47
niceness 184–5
Nielsen 153
NIMH (National Institute of Mental
    Health) 47, 48
'no', saying 92, 181
Notonthehighstreet 65
number crunching 208
nutrition 34, 52

O
obnoxious behaviour 126
obsessive compulsive disorder
    (OCD) 42

Olins, Alice 126, 127
Oliver (son) 10, 18, 25, 29, 89, 110,
    212
    birth of 7, 17, 41–2, 43–4, 87, 111,
        142
    separation from 27, 89
Oliver, Jamie 193
oneself, knowing 129
online businesses 1, 30–1, 67,
    72–81, 117, 152–78, 208
opinion 71
opportunity, how to seize 86
optimisation 166–7, 193
Ordinary Maternity Leave 29
outer critics, how to silence 95
outsourcing 11
over-delivery 168
oxytocin 40

P
page authority 166–7
pampering 56–7
Papa G (father), *see* Psarias, George
parenthood 187 (*see also*
    fatherhood; motherhood)
    boring nature of 115
    and career 20, 65, 106, 110–15
    first-time 8, 7, 14, 17–18, 20–6,
        41, 63
    how it changes you 110
    misconceptions of 21, 23
    unpredictable nature of 21
parenting skills, and work 106–7
Parry, Steve 9
part-time work 3, 28, 64, 65, 87, 93,
    142, 149, 176
passion i, 12, 13, 16, 19, 30–1, 61–4,
    68, 72, 79, 83, 89, 94, 95, 105–35,
    156, 180, 181, 192, 203, 205, 207,
    212
past, learning from 97–8
Paterson, Jacqui 66–7, 213
patriarchy 62–3, 100
PCOS (polycystic ovary syndrome)
    27, 32

perseverance 182–3
perspective 33, 64, 67, 79, 127, 156,
    167
Peter (husband) 18, 24, 46, 47, 60,
    112, 121, 144–5, 151, 157, 212
    first-time fatherhood 26, 32,
        33, 43
    Vicki meets 27
Pine, Karen 91, 100
Pinterest 77, 164, 182, 185, 201
planning, importance of 92
platform, choosing 157–8
Playing Big (Mohr) 62, 89, 109
PMS (premenstrual syndrome) 23,
    140
PMT (premenstrual tension) 124,
    139, 202
PND (post-natal depression) 29, 30,
    42, 50, 64
podcasting 166, 188, 201
polycystic ovary syndrome (PCOS)
    27, 32
Poole, Eve 68–9, 96
post-natal depression (PND) 29, 30,
    42, 50, 64
post-partum psychosis 42
post-traumatic stress disorder
    (PTSD) 29, 42, 49
PR 3, 67, 73, 80, 161, 163, 165, 168–9,
    171, 178–9, 192
    publicists 187
pre-parenthood 21
pregnancy:
    bathing during 55
    benefits of 139–40
    empowerment of 36, 53
    and importance of aftercare
        51–2, 53, 55
    liver condition, *see* ICP
    mind and body changes during
        34–9
    nesting mode 57
    second time around 52–3, 113
premenstrual syndrome (PMS) 23,
    140

premenstrual tension (PMT) 124, 139, 202
press, liaison with 169–70, 185, 189
The Princess Diaries 68
prioritising 26, 110, 112, 136, 138–40
PrizeFinder (theprizefinder.com) 170
Problogger.com 73
procrastination 96
#proudinmybikini 36
Psarias, George (father) 16, 46, 47, 59, 123, 180, 207, 211
    MBA studies 180
Psarias, Solos (brother) 22, 211
Psarias, Vasoulla (mother) 15, 16, 44, 46, 56, 127, 129, 162, 180, 211
    career 6
PTSD (post-traumatic stress disorder) 29, 42, 49
publicity 178–9
punctuation and grammar 108
Purple Cow (Godin) 152
purpose 71
Pylas, Sarah 32

R
Radio Times 8
ranking, optimising for 166–7
rates:
    how to choose 165–6
    when to increase 169
reaching out 94
reading, benefits of 57
real-time conversation 159
rebirthing 77
#Reclaimyourlunchbreak campaign v
Red v, 11, 88
Red Hot Women Awards v
Redbus 180
Reeves, Michelle 29–30, 213
regrets 207
rejection, how to handle 183
reliability 168

repeat work 167–9
repetitive action 134
resilience 71
Rhimes, Shonda 205
Richmond Park 39
Rifts 10, 16
Roundhay Park 22
Royal College of Psychiatry (RCP) 42
The Royle Family 54
rule-breaking 161–4
Ruth (friend) 39

S
salmashah.com 159
Sandberg, Sheryl 100, 102
savings 93
scoping 117
search-engine optimisation (SEO) 19, 86, 157, 162, 166, 178, 184, 187, 191–7
    offsite 198–199
    and social shares 199
self-aid kit 48–9
self-belief 2, 61, 62, 67–9, 102, 153
self-care 55, 94
    importance of 51–2, 53
self-congratulatory success 138
self-consciousness 155
self-doubt 7, 59–60, 61, 76, 99, 100, 104, 131, 133, 140
self-esteem 39, 95
self-expression 7
self-hosting 167, 193
self-promotion 179
self-reflection 122, 135, 208
self-validation 208
self-worth 40, 95, 100, 122, 150
sensitivity 102, 121, 125, 139
SEO (search-engine optimisation) 19, 86, 157, 162, 166, 178, 184, 187, 191–7
    offsite 198–199
    and social shares 199
Sex and the City 23, 40
Shah, Salma 159–60

ShapeShifters 38
short films 10, 16, 17, 34, 133
The Simpsons 8
Sketchy Muma 30
Sketchy Muma (Lewis) 31
Sky 99
sleep 204
    how to aid 133
    necessity of, during pregnancy 21, 56
sleep-deprivation 1, 37, 111, 125
smuggies 24
Social Blade 169
social media (*see also* social-media handles by name):
    ads 178
    downsides of 56, 81, 86, 163–4, 207
    etiquette 184
    growing your business through 73, 75, 76, 142, 147, 156, 162, 183, 185
    no-no's 185
    obsession, danger of 207
    as real-time conversation 159
    reasons to embrace 8, 199
    targeted ads 178
    upskilling 64
    verification ticks 177
SocialOomph 164, 170
Sorted (McGrattan) 107
spamming 172, 185, 198
'sparkle' 10
Sparrow 206
Speak Up Like a DIVA (sholakaye.com) 76
Spice Girls 12
spike 71
sponsorship 9
stargazing, calming effect of 57
Statutory Maternity Leave 29
stay-at-home dads 3
stay-at-home mums 29
Step Up Club (step-up-club. net) 126
Stewart, Maryon 139–40

strategy 13–14, 84–5
stress 7, 39, 46, 68, 90, 125, 130, 134, 136–8, 146
    disorders 29, 42
    how to limit 118, 150
Stylist v, 13
subjectivity 128, 208
success, traps of 207
Sugar, Alan 126
Suits 40
Sunday Times 99
Super Lucky (superlucky.me) 171
Supermum, myth of 137
Susanne (blogger) 49
switching off 163–4

T
Tailwind 164
taramohr.com 89
Tavender, Ursula 57, 146–7
tax 172, 174–8 *passim*
tech, choosing content 153, 157
Thompson, Andrea 209
Thompson, Kate 99
Thorpe, Harriet 75, 122, 213
thought leadership 152, 183–4
time out 86, 134
time-out 205
timing 95
tips, *see* top tips
title tag 197
Tomczak, Sarah 88–9
top tips 26, 109, 140, 196
    accounts 176
    business planning 92–4
    co-parenting 50–1
    comparison paralysis 84–6
    confidence 96
    criticism, how to handle 126–30
    financial 153
    juggling 150–1
    marketing 3
    passion for 130–2
    PR 3, 180–6
    repeat work 167–9

returning to work 90–2
rule-breaking 161–4
self-care 49, 56–8, 202
tech 153, 157
vlogging 155
work space 145–9
YouTube 157
trading styles 174
trauma:
    birth 41–2, 45, 50–2
    dealing with 123–4
    moving on from 52–3
Tribe (Godin) 152
trolling 13
trolls 13, 105, 121–30, 206
'true north' 96–7
Tupperware parties 8
'Turning Passion into Pounds' v, 13
Tuxford, Nic 164, 191–3
Twitter 161, 163, 164, 169, 184,
    200–1, 209
    Follow and RT competitions 171
    press liaison via 169–70, 185
    retweeting (RT) 80, 171, 209
    trending 13
    village 18

U

unique selling point (USP) 74–5,
    181, 197–8
untruths, how to deal with 121–30
Urban Swim Festival 9
USP (unique selling point) 74–5,
    181, 197–8

V

vaginal birth after a caesarean
    (VBAC) 53
Vaish-Taylor, Nomita 120
Vanilla Ice 208
VAT 177–8
VBAC (vaginal birth after a
    caesarean) 53
verification ticks 177
viral content 185–6

Virk, Manjinder 112
visibility 3, 171, 179, 182, 183, 187,
    189, 200
visualisation 57, 94
vital statistics 169
vlogging (see also blog(s)/blogging):
    for beginners 155–8
    being yourself when 156–7
    content, choosing 156
    'parties' 171
    traffic 155
Vogue 11

W

What's Next Vlog (whatsnextvlog.
    com) 75
widgets 170, 171
Willingham, Sarah 116, 147
Winfrey, Oprah 205
Wogan, Terry 212
Woman v, 11
WordPress 73, 76, 193, 197
work 87–90
    after becoming a parent 20, 65,
        106, 110–15
    charitable 7, 12
    collaboration 77–81
    confidence in 87–90
    deciding what you want from
        142–4
    finding passion for 95
    importance of space for 145–9
    keys to success 70, 71
    and motherhood 28–31
    mum-powered 65
    part-time 3, 28, 64, 65, 87, 93,
        142, 149, 176
    pivoting 115–20
    reasons to return to 60–4
    repeat 167–9
    self-employed 64
    'standard day job' 20, 137, 143,
        146, 152
    structure 88
    tips for returning to 90–2

work–life balance 14, 63, 66, 106, 136, 138, 145, 205
working essentials 147

Y
Yoast 193, 195, 197, 198
yoga 56, 115, 134, 151, 205
Yoga with Adriene 56
'You Are Not Alone' 53
'you' time 3, 57, 85–6, 151
yourdiyfamily.com 120

YouTube 44, 56, 73, 142, 151, 153, 154, 155, 157, 158, 163, 170, 179, 200
YouTube Creator Academy 73, 157

Z
Zak (auntie) 137, 206, 215–16
Zeffirelli, Franco 206
'zero to hero' 153
zombie-like fatigue 23